CROSSING INTO CANADA

CROSSING INTO CANADA

STORIES FROM TWO GENERATIONS OF US WAR RESISTERS

EDITED BY
ALISON MOUNTZ

Published by

University of Alberta Press
1–16 Rutherford Library South
11204 89 Avenue NW
Edmonton, Alberta, Canada T6G 2J4
amiskwaciwâskahikan | Treaty 6 |
Métis Territory
ualbertapress.ca | uapress@ualberta.ca

LIBRARY AND ARCHIVES CANADA
CATALOGUING IN PUBLICATION

Title: Crossing into Canada : stories from two generations of US war resisters / edited by Alison Mountz.
Names: Mountz, Alison, editor.
Description: Includes bibliographical references and index.
Identifiers: Canadiana (print) 20250159805 | Canadiana (ebook) 20250159813 | ISBN 9781772128284 (softcover) | ISBN 9781772128369 (PDF) | ISBN 9781772128352 (EPUB)
Subjects: LCSH: Americans—Canada—History. | LCSH: Vietnam War, 1961-1975—Draft resisters. | LCSH: Afghan War, 2001-2021—Desertions—United States. | LCSH: Iraq War, 2003-2011—Desertions—United States. | LCSH: Canada—Emigration and immigration. | LCSH: United States—Emigration and immigration.
Classification: LCC FC106.A5 C76 2025 | DDC 971.004/13—dc23

First edition, first printing, 2025.
First printed and bound in Canada by Houghton Boston Printers, Saskatoon, Saskatchewan.
Copyediting by Audrey McClellan.
Proofreading by Kirsten Craven.
Maps by Trina King.
Indexing by Judy Dunlop.

University of Alberta Press is committed to protecting our natural environment. As part of our efforts, this book is printed on Enviro Paper: it contains 100% post-consumer recycled fibres and is acid- and chlorine-free.

GPSR: Easy Access System Europe | Mustamäe tee 50, 10621 Tallinn, Estonia | gpsr.requests@easproject.com

University of Alberta Press gratefully acknowledges the support received for its publishing program from the Government of Canada, the Canada Council for the Arts, and the Government of Alberta through the Alberta Media Fund.

Canadä

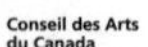

This book is dedicated to all who have survived war, and all who have resisted it, across generations and borders. May their acts of courage and conscience be remembered. This book is also dedicated to Lee, war resister and tireless advocate, who gave so much of himself to support resisters in search of refuge in Canada.

Contents

Acknowledgements

I AM GRATEFUL TO SO MANY PEOPLE whose generosity and support made this book possible. I hold deep respect for those who provided their stories for the book, and for those who contributed to the research but whose stories do not appear here. I find hope, inspiration, and love between and beyond these pages, all of which sustained me and my collaborators through this work.

Thank you to the many students and colleagues who supported this project along the way in myriad ways, including Jacque Micieli-Voutsinas, Antonia Romanisin, Kira Williams, Ana Visan, Kate Motluk, Shiva Mohan, Margaret Walton-Roberts, Kim Rygiel, Sean Lockwood, Suzan Ilcan, John Ravenhill, Ann Fitz-Gerald, Simon Dalby, Lucy Luccisano, and other colleagues at the Balsillie School of International Affairs. I also thank Tara Vinodrai, Rachel Silvey, Emily Gilbert, William Walters, Win Curran, Roberta Hawkins, Cetta Mainwaring, Helen Watkins, Celine Park, Momin Rahman, Jessica Fields, Linda Homeniuk, Raul Pacheco-Vega, Michel Hogue, and John Hagan.

Special thanks to collaborator Lisa Molomot, director of the documentary film *Safe Haven* (New Day Films), where some of these stories are told in shorter form on camera.

Members of the War Resisters Support Campaign were a tireless inspiration and so supportive of this work. I appreciate their courage in fighting for so long to support resisters and am grateful for our shared belief in the importance of documenting the Campaign for future generations and future struggles for social justice. I especially thank Michelle and Christine for their willingness to support this research and to speak with many audiences over the years.

I thank the thoughtful, dedicated, creative team at the University of Alberta Press, especially Michelle Lobkowicz, Cathie Crooks, and Duncan Turner, who shepherded the manuscript into print with care and patience.

I am also grateful to Trina King for making the maps in this book. All the maps use base data adapted from Esri basemap layers and Government of Canada datasets, with individual journeys based on materials and information collected during field research.

The research behind this collection of oral histories was funded generously by Insight and Connection grants from the Social Sciences and Humanities Research Council of Canada; the Canada Research Chair in Global Migration; the US-Canada Fulbright Program, which supported Lisa Molomot's time in Ontario; the Balsillie School of International Affairs and the International Migration Research Centre at Wilfrid Laurier University; and the University of Toronto Scarborough. Portions of this manuscript were edited at the Helen Riaboff Whiteley Center at Friday Harbor Labs.

1 Introduction

IN THEIR CELEBRATED DOCUMENTARY SERIES *The Vietnam War*, about the United States' role in war in Vietnam, Cambodia, and Laos, filmmakers Ken Burns and Lynn Novick leave out a crucial part of the story: What happened to the 100,000 American citizens who fled to Canada during the 1960s and 1970s while war raged? Among these people were draft resisters, anti-war activists, conscientious objectors, and traumatized soldiers who went AWOL (absent without leave), making the heart-wrenching decision to leave not only the front lines of Vietnam and the militarism of American society, but also family and friends. Today, many Americans in the generation who lived through the war know *of* people who fled to Canada and are familiar with the idea of emigrating north as a common consideration. Yet most know little about what happened to people once they left the United States.

In Canada, in contrast, this particular history of war resister migration is better known. The arrival of American resisters is memorialized, even mythologized and celebrated as a defining moment in the history of a country that self-identifies in oppositional terms when comparing itself to its neighbour. Canadians often imagine their country as a more welcoming, more open and inclusive, less war-inclined society than its southern neighbour. Even when reality departs from this self-image, Canadians see their country as a refuge. Given the significant number of young, draft-age immigrants entering Canada during a relatively short time, most Canadians grew up knowing people in their communities—neighbours, teachers, and community leaders—who came from the United States during the war. Popular memories of this history eventually fuelled support when a new generation of war resisters began arriving in Canada in 2004, following in the footsteps of the earlier generation's northbound journeys in search of refuge.

Through compelling and diverse personal narratives, this book documents two generations of war resisters who escaped from the United States and made a bid for freedom in Canada, as well as the people who supported them. The war resisters whose stories fill the book fled from the United States to Canada in search of safe haven during two historical periods: the 1960s and 1970s when the United States was fighting in Vietnam, and the early 2000s during US-led conflicts in Iraq and Afghanistan. This collection presents first-hand accounts of war resisters' journeys to Canada, detailing the complex emotions and moral dilemmas they faced, while offering rich insights into their motivations, decisions, and experiences. By focusing on this less-discussed aspect of US-Canada relations, war resistance, and migration histories, the book provides an inside look at how people resist war, cross borders clandestinely, and forge refuge.

Indeed, from Black Americans fleeing slavery to conscientious objectors fleeing participation in World Wars I and II, Canada has a long and complicated history as a safe haven for people leaving the United States. Today, some one million US citizens live in Canada, many descended from these historical migrations. During the prolonged conflict that the United States initiated in Vietnam, Canada offered safe haven to US citizens who were war resisters fleeing mandatory conscription. While there was by no means homogenous or unified support for resisters in Canada, in 1970 Prime Minister Pierre Trudeau famously remarked that "Canada should be a refuge from militarism" (*Toronto Daily Star* 1970). During this time, some 100,000 resisters arrived, and about 50,000 stayed, settling in their new home (Hagan 2001b, p. 3).

More recently, according to the War Resisters Support Campaign (WRSC or the Campaign) that helped them, some 300 US military personnel arrived as war resisters, fleeing tours in US-initiated conflicts in Afghanistan and Iraq to seek refuge in Canada. Approximately 50 people among this second cohort made refugee claims but eventually faced rejection, deportation—and imprisonment for those forcibly returned to the United States. While the Vietnam resisters secured safe haven in Canada as a legal form of belonging, this new generation did not (with the exception of about fifteen people granted permanent residency on humanitarian and compassionate grounds). Although largely denied legal status, evidence shows that members of the recent cohort *did* collectively find and forge safe havens *beyond* legal status, such as shelter, survival, refuge in churches, and the Campaign.

These important historical migrations connect Americans and Canadians who lead proximate and intertwined lives. It is essential to document and understand these migrations now, as the older generation ages but still has living memory to share with a society that faces the prospect of continued involvement in wars around the world. Younger generations were not alive during the Vietnam War, and the knowledge of those who lived the history, who are now mostly septuagenarians, must not die with them. This history lends insights into Canadian and American politics, identities, and cultural differences, revealing how societies change over time. Juxtaposing these two searches for protection and their disparate outcomes exposes shifting political landscapes in both countries.

This collection of first-person narratives preserves the rich intimate histories of these two historical migrations through the words and stories of resisters and their supporters. Today, people remain interested in the earlier generation of US resisters who came to Canada during war in Vietnam, yet they tend to know less about the more recent generation of resisters who came during tours in wars in Iraq and Afghanistan. Through oral histories, resisters and activists recall their journeys to and lives in Canada. These storytellers share important yet often overlooked details about their decision-making and passages to Canada as they settled in and learned to navigate a new society. These are stories replete with tension and conflict but also hope, as individuals explain how they struggled to make life-altering decisions and create new lives.

LANDING IN A CHANGED POLITICAL LANDSCAPE

Mandatory conscription—the draft—was a key feature of both American participation in the war in Vietnam and decisions to resist that war. All men between the ages of 18 and 35 were required by law to register. A lottery of numbers based on birthdates was drawn and listed in the daily newspaper, inspiring anxiety and fear among a generation of young people waiting to hear if their number had been called, which meant their luck was up.

In the histories shared here, you will learn how this generation of men tried through various means to delay being sent to the front lines, whether by invoking deferment categories assigned for various reasons, such as medical problems or psychological reasons (including sexual identity), or by belonging to a traditional pacifist organized religion. The pursuit of higher education offered a deferment category that young people with the financial means commonly pursued: as long as they were actively enrolled in university and achieving academic success (specifically defined in terms of grade point average or GPA), they could defer until graduation. This deferment became compromised, however. As the war dragged on and the need for soldiers intensified, this deferment category was only available to those who maintained above-average grades in university. Over time, other avenues for deferment from the draft were also constricted.

Half of the resisters who moved to Canada during the war in Vietnam were women, and they are present here too. You will read about their independent decision-making, leadership, and activism, as well as how they aided and accompanied the men on their journeys.

» People commonly differentiate between the experiences of the older generation, subjected to the mandatory draft, and the younger generation of resisters who enlisted voluntarily in the US military. Many of the recent cohort enlisted during the immediate aftermath of the 9/11 terrorist attacks on US soil in 2001, which led eventually to the global war on terror. Once soldiers were on the front lines, whether they had been drafted or enlisted voluntarily, their perspectives changed. While members of the younger generation were not drafted, these soldiers, like their predecessors, felt they had few options but to enlist. They believed they were lied to about their options within the military and therefore tricked into war. They also grew disillusioned and fatigued. As one contributor, Joe, notes, "No one can know the realities and horrors of war until they have experienced it."

At the height of these conflicts, there were some 340,000 American military personnel on the ground in Iraq, Afghanistan, and surrounding regions, not to mention soldiers from other countries who entered as part of a coalition to fight the global war on terror (Otterman 2005). This included Canadian soldiers in Afghanistan, and Canadian citizens enlisted in the US military. Sustaining such large forces with a voluntary enlistment policy required creative manoeuvres on the part of the US federal government. For example, the "stop loss" policy, buried in small print and bureaucratic language in the enlistment contracts signed by soldiers, required them to return to active duty for successive tours in times of war. This meant that soldiers dealing with post-traumatic stress disorder or PTSD were often surprised to find themselves returned quickly on repeat tours when they thought they were about to experience a break from the front lines.

In this collection of stories, resisters from the younger generation problematize the notion that contemporary enlistment is "voluntary." They talk about the few paths or choices available to them, which causes some people to refer to contemporary enlistment as an "economic draft." This is evident in the reasons Iraq resisters gave for enlisting in the first place: most indicate it was to access a livelihood, health insurance, and education. To outsiders, the absence of mandatory conscription differentiates the two generations, yet there are many parallels that make their experiences similar to those of the previous generation, as you will read in their histories.

» Support for draft evaders and deserters during the war in Vietnam was not homogeneous or guaranteed in Canada; resistance was controversial then and remains so today. However, many people who came to Canada did eventually find a new home. There were vast networks of support among members of civil society, from church groups and anti-war or peace movements to a highly organized, cross-border draft counselling movement. This counselling movement took hold on university campuses across the United States and connected would-be emigrants to committees and organizations in Canada that supported them in finding work, shelter, community, and, eventually, legal status in Canada.

The impact of 100,000 people emigrating to a country with a relatively small population—about 21 million in 1970—meant that Americans became an important part of the fabric of Canadian society, whether they started off in alternative communities on the west coast and in the interior of BC, as some storytellers in this book did, or integrated quickly into the life of Canadian cities like Montreal, Toronto, Vancouver, and Edmonton. While support was never guaranteed, and never unanimous, it was available, making this migration possible through small social movements fuelled by broad coalitions (Hagan 2001b). The earlier generation of resisters generally found refuge in Canada.

But Canada had changed by 2004, when the new generation of resisters began to arrive some 40 years later. The new social movement was led by the War Resisters Support Campaign—an activist group emerging from Toronto and led by Vietnam-era resister immigrants. With chapters in several cities from coast to coast, the older generation devised ways to assist the younger generation to seek refuge in Canada. History seemed to repeat itself, as the global war on terror brought with it a new round of militarism in the United States and another round of devastating deaths of soldiers and civilians.

This time, however, the newer generation of resisters met very different outcomes in their search for safe haven. Of the estimated 300 US military personnel who sought refuge in Canada as part of their resistance to wars in Afghanistan and Iraq, approximately 50 made refugee claims. Most eventually faced rejection, and some were deported and imprisoned—a personal and political history shared here in the story of Robin, the first US war resister who was deported in 2008 and imprisoned in the United States. Ultimately, only fifteen were allowed to stay.

When the US initiated these wars, there were massive protests around the globe. As this book goes to press, veterans and others are marking the 21st anniversary of the beginning of the war in Iraq. At the same time, the war between Russia and Ukraine has passed its third anniversary, and more than 80,000 people have died in Gaza (Fieldhouse 2025). Citizens around the globe must once again, and perpetually, consider how to engage and respond to new and ongoing conflicts, whether through participation, protest, support, or refugee resettlement.

CANADA AS SAFE HAVEN? THE HISTORY OF THIS PROJECT

This research was funded by the Social Sciences and Humanities Research Council of Canada as "Canada as Safe Haven? The Migration of War

Resisters from the United States." This research documents a shared, cross-border history that is at once political—a story about war and resistance to war—and deeply personal, as these politics made their way into every household in the United States and stretched across the generations with the implications of the decisions that young people made at the time. As an immigrant who moved to Canada from the United States and as a scholar who researches migration, I always wanted to learn more about this history to more profoundly understand the country that has become my new home. These histories of resistance must be documented for future generations, lest they be forgotten.

To this end, the research team conducted archival research and collected oral histories to document and share resister narratives. Oral histories have been described as prolonged conversations that disrupt hierarchies of power between researcher and participant, inviting people to tell their own stories in their own terms, sometimes across multiple sittings, and with minimal intervention by interviewers.

We collaborated with the WRSC and include accounts from two of its leaders—Michelle and Lee, both contributors to this book. The WRSC started in 2004, following the arrival of Jeremy Hinzman, the first resister of the younger generation, who came with his family that year. The WRSC was largely run by the older generation of resisters who arrived in Canada during the US-led war in Vietnam. They formed solidarity across a wide, intersectional swath of Canadian society with shared interests in fighting against war, working for peace, and supporting this generation. They were pacifists, feminists, war resisters, labour organizers, anti-war activists, socialists, and other citizens motivated to participate because of their religious beliefs.

When research began in 2016, I approached the WRSC to ask how we could collaborate. Several years into their campaign by that time, they were working to support the small group of resisters who remained and were still fighting for permanent residency and to find livelihoods in Canada. I had received funding from the Social Sciences and Humanities Research Council to support "Canada As Safe Haven?"—a portion of these funds were used to support several research assistants, including a war resister who worked as a research assistant on the project and on the 2020 documentary film about this history, *Safe Haven*. Importantly, students and resisters collaborated in the research along the way.

Alongside the collaboration with the WRSC, there were two primary research methods: archival research and oral histories with resisters and activists. While I met many activists and resisters through the WRSC, I also met others using the snowball method of referrals through friends and participants.

The research team collected these stories using the tools and techniques of oral histories. Oral histories facilitate discussion of events that unfold over a long time period, with attention to context and narrative construction. This approach preserves subjective experiences and emotions, which provide rich, nuanced insights into the past, contributing valuable layers of context and meaning that traditional records alone do not provide. Importantly, oral histories allow for the capture of personal memories and perspectives that might otherwise go unrecorded, allowing researchers to document voices often overlooked in historical records. With "a basic dynamic of two people sitting and talking about the past" (Sharpless 2006, p. 38), oral histories allow for a combination of agreed-upon topics and flexibility in the shared telling. Adding depth to historical understanding of past events and transformations, this method of data collection is especially important in preserving histories, as it ensures that personal accounts, along with their emotions, motivations, and values, are accessible to future generations.

The recorded oral histories probed migration journeys, beginning with discussion of childhood, adolescence, and the circumstances surrounding the decision to enlist or resist the draft and, eventually, flee to Canada, followed by the process of making arrangements and crossing the border. We asked people to recall their journeys to, but also their life in, Canada, from early experiences and applications for status to finding and forging new homes, relationships, and communities. Some storytellers stayed in Canada, while others returned to the United States, whether by choice or by force. In the conversations, we explored the roles played by Canada in the geographical imagination as potential safe haven prior to migration, and its place years or even decades later in their lives. Some research participants were reflecting as septuagenarian pensioners and retirees some 40 years after emigrating, while others were younger adults in their 30s who were still working as more recent immigrants to establish lives and families in Canada.

I chose oral history as a method because of the freedom and individuality allowed in the telling of one's own story. These oral histories were recorded in British Columbia, Alberta, Ontario, Arizona, Washington, and Colorado. Although I guided the tellers with a few prompts to explain something about their youth and the context in which they made the decision to come to Canada, the primary role in the collection of oral histories was to listen. Oral histories happened across one or two sittings, ranging from a total of 90 minutes to three hours. They were recorded, transcribed, edited, and coded.

These histories were edited to present them in the chapters that follow in the original words and voices of people who shared their histories. The edited stories were then sent to the tellers, inviting them to edit further, discuss, or approve as they saw fit.

The histories in this collection were selected to represent a cross-section of people, while recognizing that 12 histories cannot possibly represent the full spectrum of experiences and the rich diversity of reasons why people crossed into Canada. They introduce a collective telling of a shared history that reveals both the patterns and commonalities among resisters, along with key ways that their personal histories diverge. Some of these stories bring their tellers back to the United States, whether by choice or by force of deportation. Some faced greater discrimination entering and settling in Canada than others.

This collection of narratives complements the project's extensive public engagement with the goal of bringing Canadians and resisters into dialogue about the contemporary meaning of Canada as a safe haven. This included curation of an art show in collaboration with Jacque Micieli-Voutsinas, the Just Seeds Collective, and Iraq Veterans Against War, showing the political histories of resisters and the WRSC. The show was mounted in association with a conference we organized in Waterloo, Ontario, in 2018, which brought together the two generations of resisters as well as activists, refugee lawyers, researchers, and the public.

Collaboration with the WRSC included the collective creation of an archive to be housed at the University of Toronto's Thomas Fisher Rare Book Library, alongside archives of the earlier generation of organizers during the Vietnam War–era migration. This collaboration between the research team and the Campaign was driven by the knowledge that history repeats itself, and these histories must therefore be documented for use by future generations.

The work also fuelled the creation of a feature-length documentary film called *Safe Haven* (2020, by Lisa Molomot and Alison Mountz), distributed by New Day Films and available on Kanopy, with the goal of sharing these histories as widely as possible with Canadian, American, and international audiences interested in conflict, displacement, resistance, and refugee issues. Some of the stories included in this collection are told more briefly in the film.

THE VOICES AND STORIES IN THIS BOOK

After collecting some 60 oral histories with resisters and activists from two generations, on both sides of the border, 12 stories were selected for inclusion here to be as representative as possible of people living lives differentiated by class, gender, race, faith, and sexuality. This approach ensures that the included stories not only capture the diverse social backgrounds of the resisters, but also highlight how these intersecting factors may have informed each individual's decision-making process, their paths, challenges encountered, and their eventual resolutions.

The chapters have been ordered to tell a metanarrative that reveals stages of a journey. These journeys begin with decisions to enlist or evade the draft, and decisions to desert and flee to Canada, crossing the border, settling in Canada, becoming political, seeking status, and contending with forcible return to the US. By organizing these stories in a sequence that reflects both a chronological and emotional arc, you will be able to experience the journey of war resistance as a layered, unfolding narrative.

Each history has been chosen because of features that make the story both representative and unique and interesting. While each story is driven by the highly particular individual details and idiosyncrasies, through the twists and turns of fate that shaped each resister's life, you will be able to discern themes and patterns as you read: the feeling of having been lied to by military recruiters, the impossibility of securing conscientious objector status, the challenge of having no other choice but to flee in search of survival, a better life, a life of conscience, and the associated struggles with trauma and upheaval.

This said, no decision to resist war is exactly the same. Rather, these comprise a fascinating set of shared but unique histories. You will also discover that some of the storytellers in this book know not only their interlocutors, but each other as well, having met through the long campaigns and social movements formed to support resisters on both sides of the Canada–US border. Even though some contributors of this book may be identifiable, only first names are printed in this book in order to protect identities.

While this book has opened with my voice, by way of an introduction, from here on the voices of war resisters take centre stage. Read on to learn from people's telling of their own histories, on their own terms, and in their own voices. And a brief warning to readers that at times these stories recall histories of violence, trauma, and abuse.

In a concluding chapter, I will reflect briefly on these histories, on their intimacies, their global importance, and the insights and lessons they offer the world we inhabit today. I will discuss what kind of safe haven Canada has been, historically, for resisters, and ask what kind of safe haven it might become. As the histories demonstrate, this role can never be taken for granted. With this in mind, I invite you to engage with a rich tapestry of intersectional and intersecting experiences through these incredible histories, which not only deepen our understanding of resistance, migration, and the human costs of war, but which, importantly, also offer reminders that alternative futures are always possible.

I never tire of the inspiring and harrowing stories pulsating through the pages ahead. The longer I spend with them, the more inspiration I discover in their remarkable journeys and resilience. As the US enters a new round of geopolitical instability and potential war-making, we can all take refuge and find hope in these stories.

These histories are not only about comfort and hope, but serve as a critical reminder that safe haven and peace, human rights and their protection—like freedom from violence—can never be taken for granted. We must imagine and fight for the peaceful world we hope to inhabit. The voices in this book tell us how.

Robin at home in Colorado. (Photo by Lisa Molomot.)

2 Robin

I WAS BORN IN 1984 in Boise, Idaho, where I grew up. I come from a Mormon family. I left the church at age 17 and left Boise about six months after that, in October of 2001. I went hitchhiking for about a year all over the United States and ended up at a Job Corps centre in 2003. I learned welding there and got my GED [certification alternative to high school diploma].

I was kind of a show-off back then, kind of overly proud of my intelligence. I probably didn't really belong there. Job Corps is usually people's only option to better their lives. I was just, I guess, more intelligent than most, so I kind of pushed my neck out a little bit. And that's how the recruiters got me to join the military. They showed up at this Job Corps and they kind of egged me on and gave me a challenge to take the Armed Services Vocational Aptitude Battery (ASVAB). They said, "You think you're smart. Prove it, take this test." When I scored really high, they really started to try to get me into the military. They looked at ASVAB scores and asked, "What do you want to do?"

I made the mistake of listening to them because when they showed me the tanks, I started romanticizing all the tanks going into Iraq in 2003. That was awe-inspiring. Before they give you any of the other jobs, they show these videos, romanticizing all the different combat arms specialties, like infantry, cavalry scout (Cav Scout), tank crewman, combat arms, the support arms. They want combat arms jobs more than anything. So I'm seeing these tanks, and I got drawn to them. It seemed like a really cool piece of machinery. It looked like something that was really fun. I wanted to try, so I joined them.

But I was also drawn to it because they had a high enlistment bonus: $15,000 or something, which to an 18-, 19-year-old kid, that's a lot of money. They don't tell you they're going to take like $5,000 in taxes out.

My biological dad passed away when I was 12. He was in the army, so enlisting was a way to know him as well. He was in the Vietnam War in '68, '69, in the Army Corps of Engineers. He got out because he was injured in a mortar attack in his second deployment. He was pretty messed up from going over there. He didn't really talk to me about it. It was more like the explosive temper and waking up in the middle of the night, having dreams and flashbacks. But I was too young to comprehend that.

My parents got a divorce when I was one. My mom remarried when I was five. I had a stepdad, a great man in my life. When my dad died, the only thing I really knew about him, besides him being a civil engineer and his job, was that he was in the military.

Growing up, my friends and I used to play guns and act like we were FBI agents and in the army, and do all this crazy stuff. So there's feelings that I had as a younger child that kind of fuelled my curiosity in joining the military as well.

When I entered basic training, everything was a contest to me, so I had a lot of fun. I actually excelled both physically and mentally. Nothing was too hard for me. I strived to be at the front of everything. I wasn't the best there, but it was a fun experience.

I don't think they ever really truly broke me down. But some of the stuff started to disturb me a little bit. The cadences that were sung about killing and blood, red blood. I blocked a lot of those out. Also, hearing that we're in Iraq because we're liberating the Iraqi people, that's what you hear in the mainstream media. But then in training we're calling them the "hajji" or "hajj," which is derogatory. We were going into the desert to "kill hajji," to "kill ragheads." That's what you're hearing in basic training. I understood where it was coming from, but I didn't know if I could be a part of it. They made it just commonplace to show prejudice. I think it's a way to break down the psyche of somebody, to have them act in a group or a mob mentality, dehumanizing a group of people because if a bunch of people are doing it, it's easier for you to do it. That's just part of the training tactics. But it didn't feel right to me. I was raised by a mother who taught that there is no room for prejudice, I shouldn't hate anyone. I couldn't think of anyone as less than human. I didn't really say anything at that time.

Then, when I left basic training, I ended up in a non-deployable unit at Fort Knox, Kentucky, the same place where I had done basic training. And immediately I thought, being there, I wasn't going anywhere. I wasn't going to Iraq. I wasn't going to participate. So I kind of had those thoughts about things that they were teaching me leave my mind.

Because once you get into the military, in, like, a garrison unit, like the unit I was in, it's pretty mundane. You go to the motor pool. It's like a 9 to 5 job. I mean, you have to wake up for P.T. [physical training], but then it's pretty much a 9 to 5 job. You know, we'd work on tanks, work in the motor pool, on Humvees. Sometimes we'd go do support for training exercises. We'd help train officers coming out of college, getting into their advanced training, and a lot of people that were going to be commanders in Cav Scout units or in tanker brigade units. We'd train them and be their drivers. We'd play the opposition force, play the bad guys, play the media, do a lot of mock war games. So we'd help train that. And we'd train ourselves every once in a while, like on firing ranges with tanks. Sometimes we would test different weaponry that the military had private contractors working on.

Whenever we'd go out into the field, training officers, I started playing the opposition force. I look a little Arab, so I would end up playing Iraqi and Afghan people a lot when we'd go out to the field. You could feel prejudice even in training from these officers. And I'd always been taught that the officers, they're the moral compass of the troops, the aristocrats on the battlefield keeping things civil, being handlers of men that have to be a little barbaric. But there is a lot of prejudice being taught. They are being trained in a manner that I didn't feel is altogether right. You know, like, shooting first, asking questions later, making sure your own men get home with no care for civilian life or property damage.

I was a driver for a particular training mission. This isn't real but a training scenario: There are reports over the radio that there is a downed Chinook helicopter, and we're in a group of Humvees with all these officers getting trained on the different positions. We come to a clearing, and you can see that there's a barn way on the other side, like a kilometre away. And there's wreckage of a helicopter, and there's two troops [two soldiers] being hung from the rafters. They're already dead. There's a group of people with AK-47s, a mass of people shooting into the air. Another group of people separate from them are walking from the side, like maybe a funeral procession of some sort. And the butter bar (second lieutenant) that's in charge of the operation, leading a platoon, he orders the others to shoot and they open fire on the two crowds with a 50 cal [50 calibre], which the Geneva Conventions say you're only supposed to shoot at equipment.

So it's a double standard for any other country to do this. However, it's fine for us. One's a funeral procession, one's a bunch of, you know, could possibly be insurgents or could be a group of angry citizens or a small group within the bigger group or who knows. The second lieutenant hasn't even investigated and just starts mowing everyone down, and then in their debriefing—usually you don't hear about it as an enlisted, however I was present—instead of saying, "Hey, you know, you just killed a bunch of innocent people. This is wrong," they're like, "There's only two Americans that are hung from the rafters and the crew of the Chinook helicopter is six. You didn't account for them. You just killed American troops." That was the only thing emphasized.

It just seemed wrong to be training the up-and-coming officers of the military to be thinking in that manner. They didn't emphasize the worst of what was committed there. It was like that life was just expendable. It didn't matter. And this training brought up those feelings: they can't brainwash me, I don't think I can participate in this.

But I realized I was participating. I was helping train these guys, and I was participating in these methods that I thought to be really wrong.

I signed a contract. That's the first thing always running through my head. I swore an oath. I have to carry this out.

I started wanting to medicate myself to not feel, and I started using drugs to leave where I was, to forget the feelings that I had: feelings of helplessness, of being alone, of being trapped in this machine that makes you sick, the isolation that it puts you into. You're trying to find an escape. You can't be friends with any of the people around you, and the military encourages you to be friends with only your fellow soldiers.

I quickly realized that that wasn't me. I didn't want to be this drug addict. So I went and talked first to a really nice, helpful chaplain, and he got me to go see a doctor at the hospital. The military put me on things I thought were horrible: antidepressants like benzodiazepines. They're pretty strong: Zoloft, Trazodone, Xanax, a plethora of drugs. I felt even worse than when I had been using illicit drugs. They were just like, "Take these. Oh, these aren't working. Take these, take these to add to this, and take this." I abruptly quit taking them. When I abruptly quit taking all the medication, I got pretty suicidal. I ate like a half a bottle of pills. It wasn't enough to kill me. It made me pretty sick.

And then, before I knew it, my commanding officer started talking to me. It was actually a first sergeant, so he's the highest enlisted personnel. He just gave me this ploy about "It's dishonourable to kill yourself, and they need bodies over in Iraq." He talked me into volunteering to go to Iraq, mainly because, I don't know, because of the problems I had with the different NCOs [non-commissioned officers] and him hearing from a chaplain that I wanted to kill myself. He was like, "Be killed over there, it will avoid the dishonour over here." Then I was like, to myself, "I don't want to fucking die." I feel trapped—even more so. A week or two later I had orders to go to Iraq. These were high-priority, short-notice orders to support occupational requirements as 2nd Brigade, 2nd Infantry in Iraq.

I had a week to gather all my stuff up and check out of the unit I was in, and then ten days of leave at home, and then to report to Fort Carson, Colorado. And then a week after that I would go to Iraq: Fallujah. That's where I would have been sent.

» I went home. I was all proud, telling everyone I was going to Iraq. Still, I don't know what I'm going to do. I ate some mushrooms with the intention of figuring out: Am I going to run away? Am I gonna hide from this? Am I going to refuse to go? Or am I possibly going to lose everyone I know and bring shame to my family and be on the run for the rest of my life?

I had dreams afterwards for two days. I had the same dream once the first night, twice the second night. This dream was of an Iraqi kid, a girl maybe 11 or 12. I was standing behind a machine gun, maybe at a guard post or a checkpoint or something, and she had this look in her eyes, like she looked thirsty. So I was giving her water. I was just reaching for it. Everyone is yelling at me to kill her, to cut her down. And then I wouldn't shoot. Then she blew up, killed me, killed people. I had her feelings. I could feel her. I don't know how to explain it in a dream. It's feelings of desperation, not of hatred. Like, this is the only thing I can do, because I'm weak, and they're strong, and they're in my land. That's the way it felt. It's like, wow, I would have felt like that if I were her. I see that little girl in me. That compelled me: I would just end up getting shot or killed or get other people killed. I couldn't participate. I didn't believe any of the manufactured reasons that were made up to go there.

So I just played along like everything's normal and said goodbye to my family and friends, and got dropped off at the airport. And I never went, never got on the plane to go to Fort Carson, Colorado Springs, never got on the plane. I asked them to get my bag off, and I left. I had my friend come pick me up and hid out in his house for two months. At that point, I officially went AWOL.

They didn't even figure out I was AWOL because the unit was deployed. They thought it was just some army mistake or whatever. And I never even checked into a unit. So I don't think I was even reported AWOL until 2005, when they finally caught up with me and they figured it out. I think they continued to pay me for almost a year and a half after I went AWOL or something like that before they figured it out.

I felt like I couldn't get a job or do anything in the United States. All I could do was hide out. I didn't like that. Then in June of '04, a group of people where I was hanging out said that they would be going to Canada, to a wedding in Saskatchewan. I was like, "Oh, boom! I'm going with you guys." I only had about $600, a tent, and a backpack. We drove in. They knew I was AWOL. There was this hippie kid. He's super proud of bringing a resister over the border.

We went through such a small border crossing in North Dakota into Saskatchewan. The US side was still pretty big. It had, like, six Suburbans and this big building. But then we're going into Canada: it's like a shack with a lady, a fax machine, and she's like, "What's going on? Welcome to Canada. Can we just see your ID now?" We showed her the IDs. And she's like, "Have a great day." That was it. It was like it wasn't even a second look. There's no checking, you know?

We started heading west after the wedding and ended up in Nelson, British Columbia, and that's where I ended up with another group of people: Americans, Canadians. They were doing this dumpster-diving documentary. They were travelling. They'd already left Tofino, BC, on Vancouver Island, and were going to film their life living off the dumpsters. I found it pretty intriguing.

They called me GI Joe. I felt accepted. We travelled east, acquiring more travellers. Some of us made it to Halifax. I made it to Newfoundland. Most of the group stayed behind in Montreal. We were 15 when we got the bus to travel west again to BC. We ripped out all the seats and converted it to run on waste vegetable oil.

I had never even left the US before. I hadn't really been anywhere else. But I met a girl while I was on this trip. That's why I ended up going to Newfoundland, and then back to Ontario where my son was born in 2005. I have a Canadian son, and I was living there in Ontario.

I loved the people. I loved that I didn't have to be paranoid about anything. I felt like I fit in with everyone that I met. I couldn't work legally, but I didn't even have to ask for money. It's like people knew that I needed money or food and were more than willing to help. I thought, Whoa, what is this? This is interesting.

I heard on public radio about Joshua Key or Brandon Hughey doing a radio interview. That was the first I heard about the War Resisters Support Campaign.

I was like, "What do you mean, there's other people like me?" They're talking about these four or five people that are up there. And I'm like, "Oh, there's five people!" I was like, "I'm not the only one here! There's five people!" I just broke down all of a sudden, I was like, "Are you serious? There's five people." Then I got all paranoid, you know? Was this some ploy to find us? Like, what is this, you know, over the radio? Is this like Uncle Sam looking for me up here, like, what's going on?

I kind of forgot about it again. Then Michael Franti was having a release party in Toronto for his film *I Know I'm Not Alone*, and I ended up going to it. I gave Michael a letter explaining who I was and what I did and that he inspired me. He shared it with the crowd and everyone cheered. As we were leaving, there were a couple of guys outside handing out flyers from the War Resisters Support Campaign. And I was like, "Hey, I heard you guys on the radio. It's pretty cool you'd be here." And they're like, "Oh, you're the war resister!" So I got hooked up with them.

I applied for refugee status in Thunder Bay, Ontario, in a tiny immigration building, while everyone else did theirs in Montreal, Toronto, and Vancouver. It takes months to get your case through. Then they hear it, and then you have to wait for months, then they deliberate. Because mine was from such a small place, it took only two or three days to process. I was done with my part before lunch. I was the only person in there. So my paperwork went through quickly.

By the time I had actually finished applying for political refugee status, quite a lot of people had applied, and Brandon Hughey's and Jeremy Hinzman's cases had already gone through. The refugee board had already said they couldn't use evidence on the legality of the war in Iraq as a basis for their case; they wouldn't be able to use that avenue for protection. So at that point, it was really proving that there were systematic war crimes. It's hard to convince a panel. You know, they were already showing prejudice. Jason Kenney was the Minister of Immigration, and there was this bad policy towards war resisters.

I became a refugee claimant, and I got a work permit. I was able to work. I worked for a volunteer program for newly graduated students, Katimavik. They go on these three-month tours in different cities: three months at a time, for a total of nine months.

Months later my work permit ran out, but I had to work. So one summer I left my young child and my partner, and I went out to BC to do some work, mainly picking fruit. Because it was piecework, where I get a bunch of cash all under the table. I was headed to the Okanagan, and I got caught. I'd been sent a letter from Immigration that said I had to be at this hearing in six days, and I didn't get it in time or hear about it until I got back. Then there's a warrant made for my arrest: a nationwide immigration warrant.

I was in Nelson, British Columbia, and I got arrested. The cop said, "Hey, you're smoking marijuana." There's three guys standing in a circle, just off of Baker Street in Nelson. I was smoking a cigarette. I ended up in jail for a week there. And then these immigration officials came. They drove me to Cranbrook and put me on an airplane. They flew me away from Nelson to the immigration building in Vancouver. They said that they were going to deport me right then and there. But a lawyer stepped in, and they put conditions on my release—like, $5,000—and this guy paid a bunch of money to get me out. I had to check in monthly to immigration officials in Kelowna, BC. I couldn't leave the province. So I ended up having to live in BC.

There's a big community that I met there. And there was actually a chapter of the War Resisters Support Campaign in Nelson for a while, because there were five resisters living there, in a tiny little town.

I started working for a moving company while I was there, and living with a family. Everything was all fine and dandy, and then one day I go to check in. I called in, in July, and they said that I hadn't called in in June. There was a warrant for my arrest, and they were coming to my location. I was pretty surprised. Why would I call in if I was running away? I was not trying to run. I checked, but for whatever reason, they didn't have a record of it. So I ended up getting arrested on July 4, the second time in six months I was arrested.

I got moved pretty quickly from Nelson to Kamloops, and then eventually ended up in a jail in Vancouver. And while I'm here, they have my stay of deportation hearing. I'm not even present at this. It cleared the way for my deportation. A federal judge in Canada said that I wouldn't face an unfair justice system, that the United States is fair and transparent, that I wouldn't be singled out for being political. And, you know, she even was bold enough to say that the worst that's gonna happen to me is a discharge and maybe a month in the brig, and nothing worse will come of it. And so I was deported on July 8, 2008.

I think I'm getting let out, but all of a sudden I'm being driven to the border. And, you know, deportation. I could've been given the opportunity to fly to any other country of my choosing and not have to go back to the States. What I did is not a crime in Canada. I was a classic unsolicited extradition.

» Immigration officials sent me across the border, back to the States, in handcuffs. They told US officials, "This is the guy you're looking for." US officials had no idea what they were talking about. Look how disorganized Uncle Sam is. First off, when they wrote out the warrant for my arrest, they wrote it for a female.

Then the US is like, "Okay." And they run a warrant check on me. And it comes up: I have no warrant. They're like, "What the fuck?" Canada says,

"You want this guy." And they're like, "Well, we don't have a warrant for him. This is weird." This is at the border: Blaine, Washington. They didn't know what to do with me. Finally, they're like, "Well, this guy's an American; we're just gonna pass him off to the Washington state troopers." A Washington state trooper grabs me, and he's trying to bring me to the jail because he doesn't want to hold me. They can't produce a warrant. So the jail doesn't want me, so back into the cop car I go.

The government finally produces a warrant for me, with the right gender, and I'm taken into custody in Whatcom County jail in Bellingham.

Within 12 or 14 hours of being there, there was a massive group of people outside the jail protesting, demanding my release. The phone at the jail was ringing off the hook, and they thought that I was some kind of security risk. At this point I had no clue of this.

So I got picked up pretty quickly. They put me in this tinted-window SUV and drove me out of there real fast because there are maybe a hundred people outside, with the power of the internet, and Bellingham having one of the longest peace vigils running ever. I think it's been going since 1964.

As I left I saw all the people. Holy crap. I thought my only hope was in Canada. But people in the United States know I'm here. There are people fighting for me here. It was a relief. It brought tears to my eyes, the highest praise.

It wasn't a deportation; it was an extradition, everything that they did. It was an extradition. I was not a criminal in Canada. I did not commit any crime. I could have gone my entire life without even being arrested over here because of the warrant issue. It shouldn't be any business of a Canadian authority to hand a United States citizen over to its government and say, "This is the guy that you want." That's not right. I never was told: "Hey, you have money, do you want to buy a ticket to France or somewhere else, you know, like go somewhere else? You can't stay in Canada. You got to go." They didn't do that.

So I am moved to some crazy jail in Buckley, Washington. Put in the drunk tank there. Really hidden city jail, you know, not even like a county jail or anything. They were hiding me real quick. While I was in the jail, some really nice old ladies down at the Lions Club made these super tasty microwave plates and actually made really good food there.

People couldn't find me there. No one could find me. Finally, a lawyer here in the US, in the peace movement since Vietnam and a Vietnam resister, found me and visited. They said, "We know where you are. We know what's going on. Just if you disappear again, just, you know, here's some addresses you need to remember, so you can send stuff to us, and we can figure out what's going on with you if you disappear again, because the military is going to come get you really soon."

All of a sudden these two guys fly in in civilian clothes, you know, with the AWOL apprehension group or whatever. And they're coming from Fort Carson, Colorado. They're not in the military. They're like, they were in the military, and now they're AWOL apprehension police officers. They fly in, they take me to the airport at Sea-Tac. We fly domestically, checking their guns, go right through security. I'm wearing a hoodie with the pockets in the front, but there's holes cut in, so I have handcuffs on. But it looks like I have my hands in a hoodie. So I'm flying domestic flights with two armed guys. We fly back to Colorado Springs, where they put me in the county jail. I'm there for four days, and then they come pick me up again. They bring me to a JAG [Judge Advocate General] lawyer, and he turns out to be kind of a bit of a quack. This guy isn't too smart. All of a sudden there's a phone call at his desk. *This* guy on the phone, he's a *lawyer*, a defence lawyer for people just like me. James Branum and this group, Courage to Resist, out of Oakland, California, put up his retainer. They do a lot of work with Chelsea Manning now. They're her main supporters. They put up the retainer and this lawyer is like, "Don't worry, I'm going to come represent you. You can say or not say anything you want to this JAG lawyer. From now on, I'm your civilian representation, if you want me." I was like, "Hell, yeah."

After I'd been in the county jail for about five days, the mail started rolling in from the entire peace movement, all the different groups and their different supporters. I was getting 100 to 200 letters a day. It was kind of ridiculous: a box of letters every day. So time went by really quickly. I was court-martialled in less than a month. Seemed like a speedy trial, a little too fast. But they were making an example of me. I'm the first one to get kicked back from Canada. So I think they expected to have this huge fight and take it all the way to trial and stuff like that. But I knew I broke the law. I was AWOL. I broke the UCMJ [Uniform Code of Military Justice]. So I was willing to accept that as my punishment.

I didn't ask to go for trial. They charged me with desertion, with intent to shirk hazardous duty in Iraq. I didn't agree with their writing. I said I would plead guilty to a lesser charge: desertion with intent to remain away permanently. It's still a five-year sentence, max. I agreed if my sentence wouldn't be longer than 15 months, I would plead guilty to the lesser charge.

So there's a thing called a quantum that goes into this little file. Then there's a sentencing hearing. You get the lesser time. And the sentencing hearing, it was pretty cool. I mean, we had Colonel Ann Wright as one of my defence witnesses (my hero). And this guy who, at the time, was AWOL from active ready reserves. We had to really plead my case, how I felt it was immoral to be sent over there, to be part of it.

The judge was super conservative. At the sentencing hearing, the prosecution played a video interview that I did with Canadian Broadcasting Corporation, where I basically called President [George W.] Bush a liar and a warmonger. After I was arrested the first time, when I had just gotten released. That was what they played at my sentencing hearing. That's been the topic of discussion in a bunch of different places, because it shouldn't have been found admissible as evidence because it had nothing to do with the crime. It had nothing to do with desertion. It showed me exercising freedom of speech. Maybe you can't do that in the military. But it had nothing to do with the crime that I was accused of.

That helped a lot of people, in their stay of deportation hearings at the 11th hour, to stay in Canada, because the defence just mentioned what happened to me and this court martial. How this evidence was found admissible. And, you know, that creates a legal basis to say that the United States *doesn't* have a clear and transparent justice system, and that you *will* be singled out for being political. Canada doesn't like that. So at least on the federal judge aspect of it, a lot of people have been able to stay. A lot of people have chosen, when they get the deportation order, to leave. But it's still just a band-aid on the problem. It allows people to stay for a bit longer.

I ended up serving 12 months and four days at the Naval Consolidated Brig at Miramar (San Diego). It's where they filmed *Top Gun*, right near the tarmac. It's kind of weird. I got arrested on July 4 and was released from prison on July 9, 2009. It was just over a year, and then a dishonourable discharge.

It's a felony, by definition, in Canada because I served a year plus a day. It's one of the arguments, my sentencing—that I would be sentenced less, to 364 days or exactly a year. But they sentenced me to longer because of the crime. I committed a crime and was locked up for this amount of time. It would bar me from entering Canada, not to mention the automatic ten-year ban because I was deported. You have to get permission from the Minister of Immigration to enter after that. It just makes it harder. Doesn't mean it's impossible. There's always a way to get special permission from the Minister of Immigration.

But I would like there to be, like, a provision made that allows all war resisters and their families, even ones that have been deported from Canada, to be allowed to come back to Canada, gain permanent residency. Because I want to be back there. I don't want to be here. You know, there's a lot of awesome, amazing people here. But I can't live in a country that would elect Donald Trump as a president.

I get to see my son periodically. There's this cool group, the Rosenberg Fund for Children. The Rosenbergs were tried for espionage back in the 1950s in the United States, and they were executed. So their children, they would grow up in foster care and adoption. But they all kept in touch with each other somehow. They were all well-to-do. And they started a fund for activists that have been targeted by the US government and their children. They pay for prison visits or music lessons or summer camp or books for college, things like that. But they give us a $5,000 grant every year for my son and his mom, who is remarried and has another child now. They come down every year. We get a grant to spend time with him every year.

» After being released from the brig, I went to massage school. I wanted to train my hands to heal from being trained to kill. It's more like my own healing. I did most of the groundwork to go to this school while I was still in prison. I chose to go live in San Francisco, also because Stephen Funk was there. He was the first person to publicly refuse to go to Iraq. He was in the Marines. He was living there, and I wanted to be a part of Iraq

Veterans Against the War, in his chapter, and join the stuff that they were doing. So I met up with all of them, and I lived in San Francisco for almost two years. We did a lot of action. We did a lot of work. We started this non-profit called Veteran Artists, where we used art to heal the war within. We created a community of artists, veterans, and activists to give a means for people that have a lot of trauma they're holding in, to express themselves and maybe connect to the general public in a way that's more visceral. All these people's stories are depressing. People really don't like to hear these stories. They want to help, they may feel empathetic, but they don't want to hear it, or they can't really handle it. Art connects so much more viscerally, the way people can feel and relate to it. It's a way to bring veterans back into the fold, back into the community.

We started doing drag. We started a thing called Make Drag, Not War. We teamed up the fiercest drag queens in San Francisco with returning veterans to have them tell the stories of their traumas through drag. Drag is supposed to be expressive, in your face, and extravagant. It's kind of the opposite of the military. So that's what it became. And then through that, Veteran Artists was made. We saw how amazing of a project it was and how it helped, how the artwork helped so much.

I eventually got burnt out on anarchist activism. I couldn't do it anymore. I secluded myself, sequestered myself up in the hills, and started growing pot. I've done that for years in Mendocino county, then I spent a year in Oregon, at a medical marijuana farm, and then moved to Seattle. Then Colorado in one of the first hemp farms.

I want to be in Canada. I don't think it's fair what they did to me. I think they should have handled it differently. They should have stuck with what the majority of Canadians felt and let us stay there. I don't know if Justin Trudeau's government is holding true to their campaign promises to help us, to allow us to all come back. I hope he will.[1]

I went through basic training, probably the same way, you know, my dad went through. I went through this stuff. And I got to do all these

---

1. During the 2015 federal election campaign, Liberal Party leader Justin Trudeau stated his support for allowing war resisters to remain in Canada. Under his leadership as prime minister from 2015 to 2025, the government did eventually allow a small group of resisters who had not been deported to stay in Canada on the basis of humanitarian and compassionate grounds. Robin, however, had already been deported to the United States.

different points in my training, in my service, kind of feeling the same things that he felt. And I felt differently, or like I had the courage to think about it. He made decisions to go over there and maybe had a chance to refuse. For whatever reason, he didn't. I saw the effects war had on him, and it played a big part in me going to Canada. In a way, I was completing the journey for him, completing a journey that maybe he didn't get to do. And I never really did see much connection—I mean, there's a lot of Vietnam-era vets that I came into contact with. And the resisters that were up there in Canada, the draft dodgers, and the Doukhobors that took them in, and all the amazing things like that. I never really made a connection between me and the Vietnam vets. Now maybe that it's some time behind me, I do see that's history repeating itself.

But I felt like I didn't want to be my father. I didn't want to go through that. I really don't want to affect the people that I would have affected, more so than me: the Iraqi people.

I don't think this journey was completed yet. And what's still to be seen, what is going to happen? It was a while before Pierre Trudeau issued that order welcoming all of the draft dodgers [in 1969]. It also took time for Jimmy Carter to grant amnesty to everyone [in 1977]. So I felt like it was still unfolding. People didn't know our generation's story yet. But now that it's had some time to unfold, our story is completed, and it's a huge dichotomy. It's so different; it's like there's no love on either side of the border now.

I know a bunch of resisters that are just here in the United States. They didn't choose to go to Canada but decided to stay here and speak out. I think I'll always keep in touch with them. I think we share a camaraderie and a solidarity with each other. I really miss the Canadian people I know, like Michelle and Lee [whose stories appear in this book]. I keep in touch more with my Canadian friends than anyone I've ever met here in the United States. I want to go back there. I feel more at home there than here.

Esther and Dave, all smiles. (Photo courtesy of Esther.)

3 Esther and Dave

(As told by Esther.)

I WAS BORN ON SEPTEMBER 4, 1942, in Goshen, Indiana. I was born to an Old Order Amish family and grew up on a farm. I learned a lot about the values of faith, the importance of family unity and also the community, and the collective good of the community.

And one of the defining factors for the Old Order Amish community is their position on war and peace. There is a long history and tradition of refusing to bear arms or to give oaths under any circumstances. I grew up with that tradition of living in peace and harmony, not only with all of our community members, but also living in harmony with the earth. On a farm, we were self-sustaining and shunned any form of technology. We had no electricity, telephones, or motorized vehicles. Everything was either horse-drawn or we used our bicycle or we walked.

The rebellion came when I felt that I had to quit school at the age of 16. I wanted more than to just get married, have a large family like all of my cousins did. I wanted to go further, and I begged and pleaded with my parents until they finally allowed me to finish high school. Then I worked as a nanny and gave my money to my parents until I was 21. At that point, a very kind benefactor, actually the grandmother of the three children to whom I was the nanny, encouraged me to go to college. There was a liberal arts college in our hometown, and of course when I was 21 I had no money because I needed to give it to my parents. She told me she would give me all the money that I needed in order to finish four years of college with a bachelor of science degree in nursing.

For four years I worked very hard, and I tried to earn as much as I could outside of that. That was a transformative experience for me, where I developed and internalized the tradition of peace and non-violence that represented both the Old Order Amish and the Mennonite church.

After I graduated, I was offered a job at Elkhart General Hospital, and that is where I met Dave. We worked together on the same unit and on the same shift, and we learned to know each other very, very well, as we would have our coffee breaks and our supper together. He was the kindest, most gentle person that I had ever met by way of males in my life and my dating experience. And he was so incredibly respectful of me.

We were in our early 20s, both just starting our lives. He had gone to Goshen College, and he remembered seeing me on campus. I stood out like a sore thumb because I was wearing my Amish dress and covering. So it would have been pretty hard to miss me.

We had started dating, and we took our days off together and had a really good time: hiking, playing tennis, going to Chicago for the day.

But then there was the reality of the draft, and I knew that Dave, being a member of the Episcopalian Church, that he could not get conscientious objector status, because he was not from a traditional peace church.

It was a really sad day when he was called for his medical, and we knew that he was going to leave for the military. His family were US Marine Corps members: his father, brother-in-law, grandfather, uncles. It was just a given that he would go into the Marine Corps after being drafted. And that's where he ended up on January 2, 1969.

For me, that was the end of our relationship, because I could not compromise my own values based on my peace tradition and continue a relationship with someone in the military.

But it wasn't very long until I started getting letters from Dave, and they were very disturbing because he outlined his struggle with his conscience. He wrote things like "All we're ever taught to do is to kill and to hate our enemy." And he said, "If love is not stronger than hatred, what is the purpose in life?" And he said, "I struggle with my conscience, I can never kill another human being knowing that I may have killed my brother as part of one global humanity." He said, "I can't go any further. I don't know what to do." And he was starting to have physical symptoms. He said he developed a blind spot when he was on the rifle range, and he couldn't see the target, and he had perfect vision when he did his medical. So for me, that was more of a psychological impediment that he was experiencing.

He had talked to the chaplain and asked again about conscientious objector status. They said no, absolutely not: you're not from a traditional peace church. He tried to explain the struggle that he was having, living with his conscience. He said it went nowhere: "Be a man. Meet your obligation to serve your country. Like all of the other recruits are doing."

I got letters from him, and I sent him several letters in reply. He never received them. That was very common. He said anyone who received anything from their family, it was usually taken away. One family had sent a package of cigarettes to another recruit, and they put a bucket over his head and made him smoke every cigarette in the pack. By the time he was finished, he was deathly ill. So those were the kinds of tactics that they used in order to simply break their will and destroy whatever remnant of humanity they had so that they could recondition and reprogram them into becoming killers. He said that happened all through basic training, and the Marine Corps basic training, he said, was the worst in terms of brutality. He said they're not allowed to hit recruits, but they paid no attention to the guidelines. They got beaten all the time. And there were a number of other stories that he told me later about the brutality, the treatment, especially in correctional custody. This was all before the first time he went AWOL.

During that time, I had been very stressed because I wasn't sure, you know, what was going to happen, whether we would have a future together or whether he would make it through, whether he would spend the rest of his time in prison because of his stance as a conscientious objector. It was a very tumultuous time.

I couldn't share this with my family. Both of my brothers, when they reached draft age or when they reached 18, they went in and registered, and they got their conscientious objector status with no problem whatsoever. For me, later on, I saw that as having an unearned right and privilege. They didn't have to sacrifice anything except for a two-year interruption in their life and going into a hospital and working in some capacity, never really having to make that decision that would affect the rest of their lives. Dave had to fight to earn the right to be able to remove himself from this situation that he could not live with, and be free with his conscience.

So it was the irony of seeing both of my brothers having a right to that unearned privilege and then seeing Dave making the sacrifices that he did in order to be free.

One morning Dave got into trouble because he stuffed his scrambled eggs into an empty milk carton. This broke a rule that you cannot take food away with you from meals. Finally he'd had enough, and he just walked away from the base. He hitchhiked to Barstow, Texas. At that point he was out of money, so he called his mother in Elkhart, and she made arrangements with the local Catholic priest to take him in so he wouldn't be arrested. She wired money, and the priest made arrangements for him to fly to Elkhart.

There were two weeks of misery for Dave. He was harassed and considered to be such a shame and a disgrace to his family. They kept saying he must go back. It got to the point where his mother finally dragged him all over. He went to see a psychiatrist. The psychiatrist said, "Be a man, serve your country. Stop being such a sissy." Dave said he'd rather die than serve in the military. He went to the priest of the church where he had been an altar boy and same story: "Don't be a coward. Be a man. You know this is a time for you to grow up."

I helped him as much as I could. We had been aware that there had been a lot of protests against the Vietnam War. A lot of draft-age men were burning their draft cards and going to Canada, but we knew very little about going to Canada.

He got to the point where he was just so sick and tired, he said, "All right, I'll go back." His mother turned him in. Two MPs came to the house, picked him up, and put him in the back of the car. Dave said they drove around the block, and as soon as they were out of sight, they stopped and dragged him out of the back seat and slammed him up against the car and did a body search. They took him to the Great Lakes naval base in Chicago, and he was there for a week before they put him on a charter plane and took him back to San Diego, where he was doing basic training. He was only there for about a week when he was put into correctional custody in a program called "Motivation," and it was absolutely brutal. He said there were beatings, and no matter what you did, you couldn't please the drill instructors.

They were in correctional custody, and it was literally like military prison. There were 15 to 20 other recruits in the same situation. They had also done some kind of infraction of the rules or gone AWOL, and were all in the Motivation program together.

It was early one morning, when they were marching back to the facility from breakfast, when they passed by the fence. Dave said he knew it was as close as he would get. It's an eight-foot chain-link fence topped with barbed wire. He had been talking to another recruit. Normally they were not allowed to talk, but as they went through some of the work they were required to perform, they were able to whisper to each other. Both said they wanted to get out at the very first chance. They were close enough, and he knew he'd probably never get closer, so he just simply removed his helmet and yelled, "Now!" He threw his helmet on the ground and ran. They had about a dozen guards around this group of 15 to 20 recruits. Everybody scattered in every direction, and the guards were stunned. They didn't know what was happening. One of them ran to get help, to get more staff out onto the grounds to round up everybody who got away.

The young man that he had talked to about escaping—Dave said he looked back after he crossed the fence, and that man was captured. But there was another one who got away, and they met outside the base and then travelled together. It didn't last long because the other young man stole some civilian clothes off of a clothesline that they had passed by. And then he wanted to hotwire a car and steal it and make a getaway. Dave said, "Absolutely not." He would not commit any kind of criminal offence trying to get away. So he went on his own and made his way to Presidio Park, and that's where my involvement came into play.

He waited until the place was deserted. He borrowed a dime. There was a payphone there, and he used that dime to make a collect call. That was about 4:30 in the morning.

I had fallen asleep that night lying on the dining room floor, listening to Perry Como's "Bless This House" because it soothed my spirit. "Bless this house, our Lord, we pray, make it safe by night and day. Bless all those who live within." That was what gave me the greatest comfort. I'm getting goosebumps right now, thinking about listening to that song and his voice like satin. That was my comfort and my peace.

I was asleep when that call came at 4:30. It was so surreal. Dave, he jumped the fence, and he was hiding. There were so many feelings and emotions at that point. Is he safe? Are they looking for him? He said there were a number of helicopters flying overhead. He told me he wouldn't be so presumptuous to think that they were out to try to find one recruit who got away, because the airport was really close by and there were always planes and helicopters taking off and landing. Their Marine base is right up against the airport. In fact, when I got off the plane, I could see the fence and I could see recruits on the other side. It frightened me. I thought, I'm so close to this evil place. My mind was racing with a million thoughts and ideas and fears and concerns, most of all for his welfare and safety.

» Of the letters that I had received, there was one letter in particular. He said, "They may beat me, they may break me, but if it takes being a Marine to become a man, then let my manhood never come." And I mean, that spoke so deeply to me in terms of the depth of his conviction and his commitment to peace and non-violence and non-violent resistance. How could I help but love this man, who had been so gentle with me and so respectful? And I thought, You know what, I can put my safety on the line as well. He needs help right now. And I can mobilize the means by which I can help him.

He told me exactly how to find him and what to do: to rent a car when I got to the San Diego Airport and follow the Pacific Coast Highway. He said, "There's a road that winds up the hills of Presidio Park to a large parking lot looking over a valley." He said, "I will be there and I'll be watching that road. As you come up that road, flash your headlights and I will know that it's you."

So that's what I did. He asked if I could bring him civilian clothes. I went over to his house, and I picked out a pair of blue jeans, shirt, a beachcomber hat because his hair was very short, a pair of shoes and socks. I didn't even think about myself. I had nothing for myself. I don't think I even took a toothbrush. Because I didn't know what to expect. I just knew that I had to put into motion everything possible to go pick him up. And I called my dad and I said, "Dad, I'm gonna ask you a question. Could you loan me some cash? A couple hundred dollars without any questions?"

He said, "Oh sure. I just happen to have quite a bit of cash on hand. I don't normally and I don't even know why I have all this cash on hand right now. But sure." He just handed it over and didn't ask a single question. I immediately got on the phone and made my flight arrangements from South Bend to Chicago, and then from there to San Diego. I packed Dave's clothes, drove over to the South Bend airport, left my car there by 8:30, four hours after I got the call. I landed shortly after the noon hour and rented a car. Not a glitch anywhere. Except I did miss the first turnoff for Presidio Park, so I had to turn around and come back.

When I got up to the top, I got out of the car and I walked around and I looked all over. I couldn't see anybody. It hit me like a brick. I said, "Oh my God, what have I done? Nobody knows I'm here. Nobody knows what I'm doing. What if he has been caught? What if he has been taken into custody? Where do I go? Who do I contact? Who do I know on a Marine base?"

Growing up in an Amish community, this was a huge culture shock. This is the first time that I had flown on a commercial plane. I was so naive that when they asked me if I wanted first class I said, "Oh sure." Growing up in an Old Order Amish community, we were so isolated from the secular world, I still see in myself there's a cultural lag. So it was like a clash of cultures suddenly. Here I am outside of a Marine Corps base, trying to rescue a deserter from this evil empire. I grew up real fast.

I just looked around. I was in a valley and the hills around me were covered with mesquite. As I was looking out over the valley, suddenly in my peripheral vision I saw this dark shadow. I looked over and there he was, running down, weaving among the bushes of mesquite. He just came running, and he said, "Let's go to Los Angeles and get a bus." He jumped in the car, and while I was driving, he was changing clothes. We stopped to throw everything in the dumpster. We bought our bus tickets to South Bend and dropped off the car, then ran back to the bus station just as they were closing the door. For the next two days and nights we rode across the western United States back to South Bend, where we got my car, and I took him back to my apartment. That's where he hid until we could make arrangements.

On April 18, Dave was all packed and ready to go. His sister was getting married that night. I had gone out to run an errand, and when I came back,

Dave was gone. And I remember coming back in and the record player was still going, so I knew it hadn't been too long since he left. That was just that feeling of emptiness and hollowness, you know? What happens now?

He knew approximately what time his friend Vern would come to pick him up, but he wasn't sure of the exact time. And I thought I could leave and be back before he actually physically left. I went to the wedding that night, and what we didn't know until afterwards was that there were plainclothes officers at the wedding. They had expected that Dave would be there and they were going to apprehend him.

After he went AWOL the second time, the military issued an APB [all-points bulletin] on him. It had a comment that anyone aiding and abetting him would be prosecuted to the full extent of the law. And they had all of his physical characteristics, but what was remarkable about that APB, which both his father and his mother received, was that they had no record of his fingerprints. When they took Dave's fingerprints when he was first inducted, he deliberately smudged them. So they would have no record of his fingerprints. So even at that time I think there was that seed of doubt: "I'm gonna be a challenge for them. They're not going to have a record of my fingerprints."

You know, when I look back, and I look at all the events that just fell into place, call it synchronicity, serendipity, whatever you want to call it. Every step of the way seemed to unfold in almost a predetermined design.

The first shift I had when I went back to work, my mother was there waiting for me. She said she had been trying to call me, and of course there was no answer. And she was quite worried and finally decided that she would go to my workplace and see if she could connect with me. I remember very clearly sitting in the back office of the nursing unit and explaining to her where I had been and what Dave had done. There, they were very supportive of his decision to declare himself a conscientious objector.

» Dave crossed the border into Canada as a visitor. This family friend had a connection with a family in London, Ontario—a couple from Great Britain who had immigrated a number of years before. They had four small children and they said, "No problem, Dave can stay with us." So they gave him a mattress on the floor, and that's where Dave slept, and they just integrated him into their family life. Which was really good because it gave him the welcome and support he needed, because he wasn't going to get support from his own family.

Sometimes people ask, "How did his family feel?" Well, he was a disgrace to the family. His mother finally came around, but his parents were divorced. And when his father died, Dave was not named in the obituary as being a son. His father had disowned him.

After Dave came to Canada, I wanted to see for myself what it was like. So every time I had more than two days off from my job, I would make that six-hour drive to London. One of the first things I did was look for an apartment where Dave could live and maintain himself and have his own space, and allow the family in London to have their own space as well.

I came to Canada in 1969. My parents have always been supportive of me and supportive of my decision to come to Canada. They understood why Dave made that choice based on the fact that he could not get conscientious objector status and that he had to look at the alternatives, which could have been going underground or going to prison or coming to Canada where we could live in peace. My dad had a truck, and we loaded all of my personal belongings on the truck, and he drove me to Canada. They often came to visit and generally supported us.

Now, one wouldn't imagine that there would be too much culture shock coming from the United States to Canada. But there was. The language. The metric system. I remember with my first job, I think I cried every single night when I came home from work. And also just establishing a network of support and community. We had no family here, we had no friends. We had to start completely fresh.

We were very conscious of the political thought in Canada. There were many people who were still ridiculing and scorning decisions like Dave's decision to not serve in the military. And so we felt very self-conscious. Also, it was a new country, we had just been married, and we had come from such a traumatic two months, at least, before we reached that point where we had been married.

After two years we decided that we would move into an unfurnished apartment and we would furnish it with the items that we wanted to see in there, and it became our own. And I see that as a turning point. We then graduated from there to a rental home, and then we purchased our own home. And that was about the time that our first child was born. We didn't have any children until after we had been married for six years. And in retrospect we would not have been ready in terms of our maturation level, our assimilation level into Canadian society, and our emotional level to be parents before that six-year mark. And that, becoming parents, was a real turning point for us. Suddenly this is our future, and our future was rooted right here in Canada. And we've lived in London ever since.

» After we came to Canada, we started getting involved in kind of a loosely knit activist network in London. Whenever there were peace rallies that were held in London, we participated, because we opposed the Vietnam War.

When a new generation of war resisters started crossing the border in the early 2000s, both Dave and I immediately said, "We're in, just let us know how we can participate in the best and most helpful way." We went to all the meetings, and then we started to learn to know each one of the resisters in a different way and a different level. In many ways we were older and more mature. Our children had gone off to university, but these young men and women reminded us so much of where we were during the draft era and during Dave's encounter with the Marine Corps. We understood completely what they were going through. And we recognized how critically important it was to be there to provide the support for these young men and women. And we were involved in every single aspect, whether it was finding an apartment or getting money or buying food or providing childcare for those families who had children. Every aspect, going with them to visit their legal counsel and just developing relationships, and relaxing, and going out for coffee.

One of the resisters who had done a tour in Iraq came to Toronto with her family. At that time, she and her husband had two children. I was working in Toronto then and became heavily involved in the War Resisters Support Campaign there. Of course my interest was very much aroused when I heard that there was a female resister. I met Kim at a number of our public rallies and many of our meetings where she spoke and shared her life story. And of course, with Kim being a mother and being a female, and me being a female and being married to a deserter as well, there developed a bond with her, especially after she became pregnant. As a mother, I could only imagine what she must have felt, especially

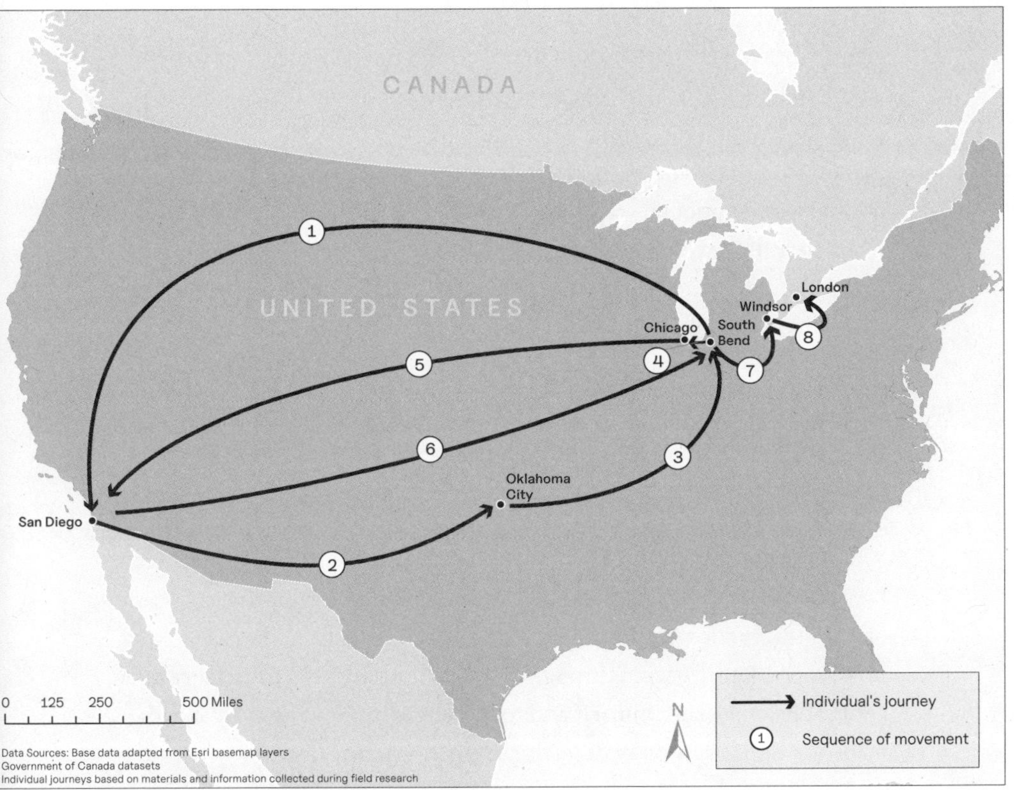

MAP 1: Esther and Dave's journey in 1969.

going to Iraq and leaving her two small children behind. So we developed a special relationship while she was in Toronto.

After she gave birth, it was so beautiful. She would have this little carrier on her front that she would carry her daughter in, and she would bring her to the public rallies, and there she was, waving her sign with this little baby—this beautiful little baby nestled in the carrier on her abdomen.

Dave and I had given her some money and also a card to simply wish her well, and all the best. After she was deported, she wrote me a letter, which came after she had crossed the border. It touched me very deeply. It was a two-page letter where she talked about all people being angels, but there comes a point in time when we forget who we really are. I heard her speak at a number of events, and she never failed to inspire me and touch me deeply. I felt a great deal of pain when I found out about the circumstances under which she was put into military prison, and giving birth to yet another child in prison and not being allowed to bond emotionally with that baby. Mothers need to bond with their children. I knew the psychological impact of being removed from the mother, and that bond failing to develop, and in turn the child not developing in a normal way emotionally or physically.

I was really deeply touched by Kim. I know that she still has belongings in the War Resisters office at the Steelworkers Hall. There have been times when I have thought if I had the means and the time, I would simply load up her belongings and drive to wherever she is and deliver them. One of them is a sewing machine. I used to see it every time I went in there. Every time I go in that office, I see all the posters on the wall, and I see all of these familiar faces.

» In retrospect, I recognize that Dave was traumatized by his experience. I see all the symptoms, now. I didn't then. I saw all the symptoms of PTSD or post-traumatic stress disorder. He had been through hell while he was in basic training. He went through hell wrestling with his conscience and being able to live with himself and to live in peace knowing that he had made the right decision in deserting from the Marine Corps.

Thinking back after 50 years, we wouldn't do anything differently.

Leah at home in the Slocan Valley. (Photo courtesy of Leah.)

4 Leah

I WAS BORN IN CROWN HEIGHTS HOSPITAL in Brooklyn, New York, in 1947. I spent my first five years living in the projects in Fort Greene, and then we moved to New Jersey when I was five. My family is Jewish, and when we moved into a very Christian suburban area, I started noticing some differences. It was an Italian and Polish Catholic neighbourhood. I was growing up noticing these differences but still participating in Jewish life. I happened to have some really good religious teachers who were committed to the portion of Judaism that speaks to social justice, and that always just resonated with me. And that dovetailed with my family's broader commitment to the labour movement and American socialism. So there was a setting that made me ripe for the civil rights movement in the early '60s, and then the war resistance movement.

My dad worked for the Defense Department. He got a job in Washington, DC, so we moved down to Maryland when I was 16. That kind of fractured my life because we left the community where I had roots. I had an opportunity to go to college on an early entrance program, where I was fortunate to be accepted. I went to this tiny college out in Mount Carroll, Illinois, with only 300 students. Everything was done in seminar, not lecture classes, and the two biggest things on campus were the Folklore Society and the civil rights movement. This was 1962, '63, and the civil rights movement was starting to really be a locomotive. And so there I was in this environment where those things were important. I was 16 going on 17, very impressionable, volatile, and passionate. And I wound up following those political leanings for many years.

When I left school, I transferred to Wilkes College in Pennsylvania, close to my parents, and one of my brothers was going to school there. My folks thought that my brother could keep an eye on me and get me back on the rails, but that was a failed experiment. I wound up leaving there to go to New York City, where I got involved in anti-war activities in 1965. Then I moved on to Southern California, and the big things that were happening there were the drug subculture, the Summer of Love, Haight-Ashbury. All of that stuff was just exploding. And the draft resistance.

My husband was draft age. We were both committed to the pacifist lifestyle we'd been learning about through the civil rights movement, and non-violent resistance. We participated in vigils and non-violent war resister movements. And eventually we got involved with what was, at the time, an underground railroad moving men along who were trying to get out of the country without being seen. I was part of a counselling movement as well as the protests. In 1967 it became obvious that the only thing to do was to leave the country. I was opposed to the war in Vietnam. I was really disillusioned with America. I couldn't reconcile American military and espionage behaviour with the narrative that I had been raised with: America the beautiful, America the great, land of the free, home of the brave. There was just this disconnect between what I had been raised to believe and what I was finding out, not just about the Vietnam War, but interference in Latin America, interference in Europe.

It just was too jarring, and I needed to get out, not just as the wife of a war resister, but as a war resister in my own right. Because it was illegal to counsel men to refuse the draft, I was in a legally vulnerable position. So I consider myself to be a legitimate draft dodger.

Because my husband was draft eligible, because we were under investigation by the FBI, our mail was being opened. Our phone was being tapped. We were followed by FBI agents as we were out doing our business. It was time to leave—for me, as well as for my husband at the time. So it was very much a mutual decision, a mutual choice. I was raring to go. I was just a 19-year-old. I was like, "Well, let's do this. What's the big deal? Just pack everything in the van and let's go."

After counselling others to avoid the draft, it was just a natural progression for me to leave for Canada. At that time, 1965 to 1967, there was so much growing resistance to the war in Vietnam. Many of us were trying to find ways to resist it effectively. And because it was military conscription, the draft, it was really urgent to come up with individual solutions: the personal is political. So many men who just didn't know what to do, they were spinning around going, "What can I do, what can I do?" The communication tools back then were not as immediate as they are now, but people talked, and people related, and people hitchhiked back and forth across the country, talking to each other, talking to other people, going, "What can we do? How can we resist this? It's not just going to vigils and protests. We need to make our men safe." Women as well as men were doing this, were sharing information on how to fool the draft medicals, on how to get out of it, how to pretend to be crazy. You know, "Eat five pounds of bananas every day and it'll screw your metabolism up and give you flat feet, and they will reject you." There were so many men, all of whom needed a personal solution. I was part of that wave of people who cared.

In order to learn how to make my husband safe, we had to learn all these other things. One of my talents has been making those connections between people and information, and putting those little bits together and going, "What if you do this?" I know the fella down the street who I hardly talked to, he's in the same situation. I'm going to tell him about it. And this woman that I met at the library who was crying because her husband is being drafted, she needs to know this. So I just sort of built on that.

My husband tried to get conscientious objector status, but it was denied. He tried to get 4F [unfit for military] medical status, but it was denied. Ultimately, we realized we had to leave the country, and the choices were Canada or Sweden. We shared this information all along, with our friends and our friends' friends and with all the little groups and organizations that were doing this. So you'd hear that, like, these guys who are out on the road hitchhiking at six o'clock on a Saturday morning, they're all trying to get to Vancouver. Let's go out there and give them a ride. Can't take them far, but we can take them from Santa Barbara to Santa Maria. Or maybe on a good day we'll drive all the way up to San Francisco and drop them off at the next informal way station, where they can connect with other people who are on the same journey and with other people who are also willing to help them. Get them out of the country where they will be safe—not just their own physical safety, but where they will not be required to go and do violence to other people. That was a really important component of the safety question. It was the ethical safety as well as the physical safety. Most of us were very moral about those choices. It wasn't just "Oh, I'm scared to be a soldier, I'm going to leave." It was "This is wrong. This is just absolutely fucking wrong. And I'm not going to do it. If I have to go to jail, I'll go to jail, but I'll try to find a different way out of it first."

We drove up from Southern California, drove up to Vancouver and then across Canada to see the country before we made that immigration commitment. In those days you could immigrate at the border. So we drove across, went to Toronto, decided that we really liked the country. We liked everything we had seen. We felt welcomed. We went back down to New York City to pack up the rest of our goods, collect a bit more money by working really hard and living with friends for free. And six weeks later we drove up to the border and said, "We want to immigrate."

I knew that Canada did not have a draft, that half of the country was English and half of the country was French. My proportions were a little bit off. It was a multicultural country that celebrated those differences rather than making everything a melting pot. And I knew that Canada in general was welcoming of American draft dodgers. Because we drove up and then drove across the country, at least we saw what there was. We never stopped anywhere long enough to really delve into the communities, but we saw the whole geography, west to east, of the southern half of the country. I felt that I knew enough about what I was getting into that I could make some rational choices—well, what seemed to be rational at the time. I liked what I saw. I liked the open spaces. I loved the smaller population, the smaller size of the cities, coming from a country where population numbers were huge, feeling that nothing I did had an effect. To come to this country where things were so much smaller that I could go, "There's only 20 million people in the whole country, my voice will be heard. I can go someplace and be an effective part of it." I didn't feel so disempowered and disenfranchised. It was all such a grand adventure at 19: "Whoa, let's do this!"

We started at Niagara Falls, where we tried to emigrate. The border guard said, "You know, I'm feeling nervous about your application. I'm not 100 percent convinced that you would be a good match for Canada. So I'm going to give you a couple of options: you can force my hand and make me make a decision, which you might not like. Or you can withdraw your application and there's no penalty for withdrawing. Maybe you can find another border station, like 30 miles down the road at Buffalo/Fort Erie, who might be more sympathetic to your situation."

So we withdrew our application, got in our Volkswagen van and drove down to Buffalo/Fort Erie, put our papers in there, and were accepted. That was August 18, 1967, and our papers were stamped in Ottawa, August 21, 1967. So when the August 21 [2017] eclipse happened, it was really a big celebration for me of—what? '67 to 2017—my 50-year anniversary in Canada, that the universe was celebrating with an eclipse just for me.

I think about that border guard so often. The fact that this fellow, this border guard, looked at our application and felt like it was a knife-edge decision for him. He didn't feel absolutely assured that Ottawa would approve it. But he didn't want to give us no hope either. And, you know, he did the kindest thing he could do, which was to say, if you withdraw your application, you can apply again somewhere else. There was a very good chance that a different border guard would approve our application. He was fine with that, as long as he didn't have to wear the responsibility himself.

There was a lot of information being shared across Canada as well. When we came to Vancouver, there was an organization of Canadians and Americans who had an office and safe houses where people could be put up when they first arrived. They were helping people arrive in Canada and giving information of where to go and how to get there.

We stopped in Winnipeg. There was a similar organization there. And these organizations also were very much connected with folk music, which was huge at the time. As a musician, that was really important to me. And then again in Toronto and Montreal, there were organizations or organized groups of young people who were saying, this was happening, we need to be part of it, we need to help keep these people safe, we're doing the right thing. So my experience of Canada was that it was welcoming and accepting of a political stance that in the United States had been so risky. And in Canada it was just like, "Pfft, no, you're safe here." It was really a relief.

We settled back east initially. I wound up settling in Montreal for two and some years, which was really neat because I got to practise my high school French and become pretty fluent in French. I loved living in a different culture, being part of a much more cosmopolitan lifestyle, but I missed being out west. However, later my husband and I split up. And about a year later he got an exemption from the draft and he did go back to the States. And he lives in the States still. I heard from him a few years ago. He said, "Oh yeah, I'm still living here and blah blah blah." But, you know, it's been so many years. We have no relationship, but I know that he did go back and stayed in America. He left America very regretfully because he felt he had no option. So when it became possible for him to go back there safely, that's what he chose to do.

I struck out on my own in Canada. I was involved in the music scene. I was in a band in Montreal, and one of the bandmates and I wound up hitchhiking across Canada, going back to Vancouver. I did some political activity along the way. I mean that's just what my life has been: community building and finding the right way of doing things.

I knew that I wanted to stay. This was my home, my decision, my choice, my move. Regardless of what this person who used to be my husband chose to do, I was staying in Canada.

A big factor was: if I ever have a son, I do not want to see him become a soldier. So it was just like there was no choice to make in that sense. I was committed to staying in Canada, and I did. I did get involved with somebody else and ultimately had a son. I was so glad that he was born in Canada and not America.

I came back west and wound up leaving the city and choosing a much more rural lifestyle. I lived in a few places around British Columbia, discovered this valley in 1971, and moved here. It was home. Together with four or five other friends at the time, and my little brand-new baby, we were driving around BC, looking for a place to buy land and start a communal farm, a little community. The Slocan Valley was one of the places we came through. There were five of us in this little Volkswagen station wagon, driving up the valley, stopping here and there, but not really connecting anywhere. We got as far as Hills, which is just 15 kilometres north of here, and there was a bank of mailboxes by the side of the road, and we stopped, and we went, "What are we doing? What are we looking for? Where are we going? Where are we going next?"

We're sitting there in the car, and all of a sudden somebody knocked on the window of the car. And we were startled, but we rolled the window down. And this long-haired hippie said, "Whatever it is you're looking for, you're not going to find it unless you get out of your damn car." He turned around and he left. He hopped in his pickup truck and drove away, and we rolled up the windows and continued up the road because we were just totally shocked. We got as far as Nakusp, just the next town up, it's about a 20-minute drive. And we stopped the car and looked at each other and went, "He was absolutely right. We're not going to find it unless we get out of the car." So we turned around and went back to the same place where this fellow had talked to us. And we just started knocking on doors until we found him. And we said, "You were right. Can we crash here tonight?" And that was it. That was it.

We wound up going back to Vancouver a few days later, getting everything, and coming back here and camping until we found land to buy. We all dispersed eventually, but for me, the experience was: I'm home. No doubt about it. This place chose me. I'm here. I'm not leaving. I still know that fellow. He was an American draft dodger as well—he and his wife and young child. He still lives here. There are a number of American political refugees up here from that era. It was a very popular place to come. It was sympathetic. The Slocan Valley has welcomed successive waves of different cultures, different nationalities: Japanese, Germans, Italians. It's just that kind of place. There is a particular energy to it. So I've lived in this valley since 1971.

At that time, many of us were political refugees, looking for a different life from living in the city. We were probably the world's most highly educated peasantry, moving out to the country with "How to build a log cabin," the book, "How to survive in the woods," the book. Like, I know we need an axe, we'd better go to a store and buy an axe. It was just very bizarre. But for those of us who embraced it, it worked. We're not as much of a community as we were back then. Because we were doing work parties and really helping each other out. And we started an alternative school and all, you know. We had a passel of kids together, who are still friends. We all still know each other, and we have that connection. That's because so many of us moved far away from our biological families. We formed a tribe. Even though we're not all individually super close, we're part of the same community, and that's very comforting. I really feel my roots are here.

I knew I was staying in Canada, and I felt that it was part of my responsibility to become a Canadian citizen if I was going to embrace the advantages and the privileges of living in Canada. I felt it was my responsibility to take on the responsibilities of being a Canadian citizen. So I signed on and I said, "Yes I do. I'm committed." It also meant that I could vote in Canada, so I could participate in that part of the common life, which has always been important to me. I mean, politics is politics where or however you categorize it: the resistance to the draft, the resistance to the Vietnam War, those were political issues. The civil rights movement was a political issue. The women's liberation movement, it was political. So it wasn't all that huge a step to also be able to say, "I can vote here. I can participate in that part of political life as well." And, in fact, I felt I had an obligation to do so. If I was gonna be a rabble rouser, I should also take part in the whole process.

I consider myself Canadian. At the time that I took my Canadian citizenship, the American citizenship law, to my understanding, said if you pledge allegiance to a foreign monarch, if you serve in a foreign military, you automatically lose your American citizenship. And I was happy about that. I said, "Queen, I'm yours. I pledge allegiance." I'm no longer American in my estimation. Several years later that law was changed in the States, to my understanding, and they retroactively applied it. All of those people who had thought they lost their American citizenship automatically, we're still considered to be American citizens. I just don't consider myself to be an American citizen. I carry only a Canadian passport. This is where I live. This is where I identify. This is where I raised my family. This is where all of my roots are now and have been for 50 years. So I'm just Canadian. I was born elsewhere. But now I'm Canadian.

I was somewhat estranged from my family for a few years. They had a hard time understanding and supporting my political radicalization. I was the black sheep of the family, politically and socially. And the fact that it was a girl who was being such a rebel was the real break that happened. At least for my mom, it was almost impossible to understand and accept. In retrospect, I can be a little kinder towards them. At the time, it was just, like, "We're fighting, I'm out of here. This is my life. They're not going to tell me how to live it." And I was pretty categorical about that. I had three

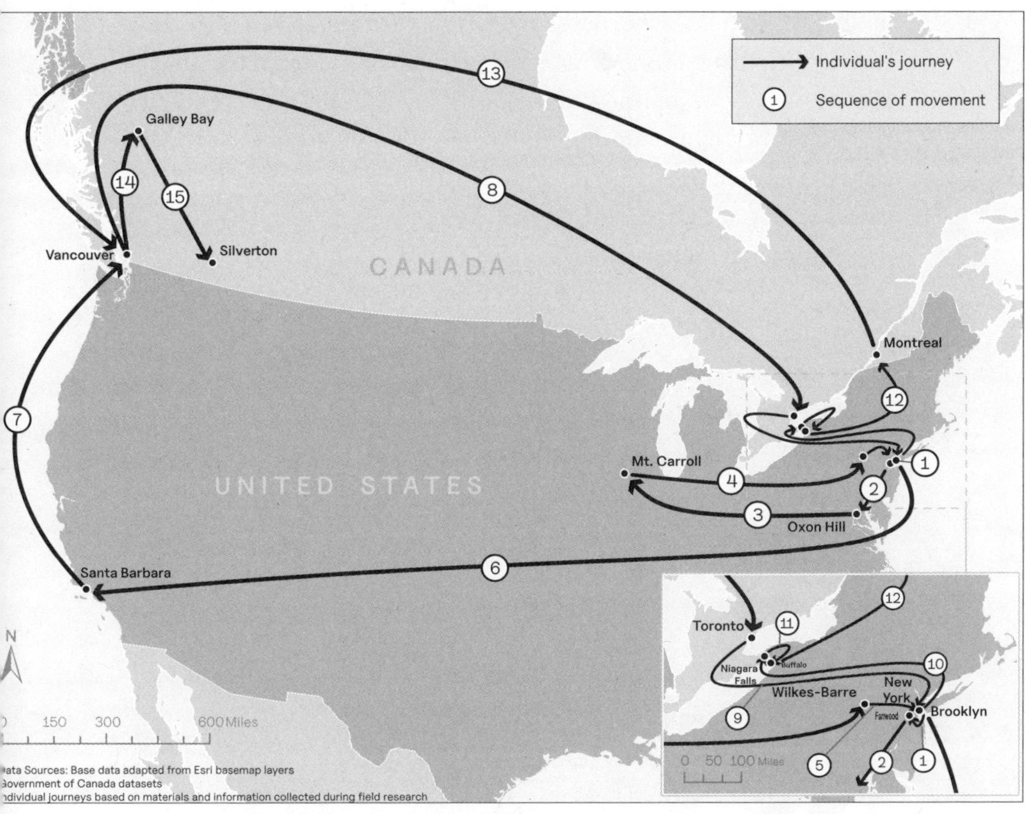

MAP 2: Leah's journey from her birthplace in Brooklyn, through her education, to her journey to Canada in 1967 and her move to British Columbia around 1970, settling in the Slocan Valley in 1971.

brothers, one of whom had enlisted in the army, and two of whom were draft eligible. I tried to convince them that they didn't have to go. They listened, but that was not their choice. They didn't see things the same way.

My dad understood a little bit more than my mom did, even though he worked for the Defense Department. He had fought in World War II. He was very patriotic, but he also used his brain. As what was happening around the Vietnam War became more apparent to him, he understood more about my choices. But, you know, they didn't really understand sex, drugs, and rock and roll the way that I did. And so, there were years that I was extremely estranged from them, where there was minimal contact by mutual decision. Over the course of time that changed, and after I had my son, they felt that it was important to find common ground rather than to carry on the antagonism. And, eventually, so did I. And we were able to create a relationship. And I think, ultimately, all of them came to appreciate and respect my independence and realize that nothing they said or did was going to change me. So it was like either accept it and have a relationship, or don't accept it and don't have a relationship.

I still come at international conflict from a perspective of "There has to be a pacifist solution. There has to be a diplomatic solution. There has to be a humanitarian solution. There cannot be a military solution." Which is not to say I wouldn't fight back if attacked. But in all of my actions, and in all of my positions, going from the very personal to the geopolitical, there has to be a pacifist solution. I just can't support military solutions.

Interestingly, I was recently at a Federation of Canadian Municipalities conference. We have an annual conference. The conference was in Niagara Falls, and my hotel room overlooked the border crossing where we had gotten turned away. And to be there as an elected government official and look down on the place where it could have been yes, it could have been no. It was just so cool.

I'm happy with my life. The only thing that drove me nuts when I first came to Canada and lived in Montreal was that there were times that the RCMP actually collaborated with the FBI in trying to locate illegal American immigrants and try to send them back. At least once, when I was in an apartment, the RCMP and FBI came to the door and were looking for very specific people who they had reason to believe were in Canada illegally. Other than that, man, I was so blissed out. It was really wonderful. I was really young. I had no idea of consequences. I was just living in the moment. And, you know, I was really fortunate that I made some good choices despite myself.

I don't know how to reconcile the way the world is right now, except by continuing to hold my position, which is that there has to be another solution. It's why I chose to be part of a group that brought a refugee family into our community, why I choose to be involved in local politics, because I can do things. It's why I work towards trying to develop deeper understanding of what has happened with the Indigenous Peoples on this continent, and the European settlers. It's why I work towards reconciliation, towards making amends for the awful things that we've all done. It's important to me to create peace, which is a dynamic of equality and justice. Tada!

Linjamin as a young recruit. (Photo courtesy of Linjamin.)

5 Linjamin

I WAS BORN IN MEMPHIS, TENNESSEE, in 1975. I grew up there until the age of five, until we moved to Lexington, Kentucky. Growing up was challenging because my mother was a single mom because my father was murdered when I was four. That prompted us to move to Lexington because the violence in Memphis was too great. So that put us in a precarious situation where we had to move. We moved around a lot. My mother was trying to find employment as a teacher. Not being able to find employment put stress on her, and she developed alcoholism as a way of coping with moving to a different city and state, not with a lot of resources. In the early '80s, it was very, very difficult. She didn't really trust many babysitters, so she left me home alone a lot. So I grew up very isolated.

I eventually ended up in the northeast. I had an aunt in Stamford, Connecticut, a suburb of New York. I went to stay there in the summer of 1988. I would usually go vacation with my aunt summertimes, because her husband had a severe accident and suffered a spinal cord injury. My mother left Kentucky to come to stay with my aunt in Stamford. And then we stayed there until I matured. That's how I ended up growing up and going to university in Connecticut.

When my mother and I moved to my aunt, she had a restaurant, but also a bar. And the fact that my mom's alcoholism was already in full progress, this really gave her kind of a licence to drink even more because it was more accessible, and it was free. So her alcoholism increased to the point that eventually she passed away. I was 14 at the time. I then ended up in "the system" or foster care. That lasted for four years, and that was a horrible experience for four years.

I was emancipated at 18 years old: an adult at 18 with no real life experiences. When you're in these institutions, your education is sacrificed. Sometimes, you know, you're with other children that are suffering from a lot of psychological issues, from the separation of parents and all different types of ills that they have to overcome. So when you get emancipated at 18, you basically have no life skills. I was just barely able to make it into college, and I know it's by a stroke of luck.

I was very fortunate to be able to go to university. It takes a normal person four years, more or less. But it took me double the time, you know, based on things that I had to overcome.

When I graduated university, I was about 26. I graduated with a degree in sociology and psychology. I initially wanted to get my doctorate in psychology and become a psychologist and help children like myself overcome some of the challenges of being in the system. But when I got out of university, the financial hardships were immediate.

Having no support, I had to find housing, I had to find a job, I had to find a social life. All these things came crashing down at one time, which made it really difficult to attain during that time. But I was able to get a job working as a direct care worker, working with children in New York, children who had difficulties. They were in foster care. They'd been taken away from their families, whether their parents died or died of HIV or they have behavioural issues or psychologically challenging issues. I did that for about two or three years. But I ran into the financial strain of living in New York City at the time. I moved to Harlem, and I was in a decent place. It was safe. That was my main concern. But the rents were unaffordable.

So that put me in a predicament where I first started thinking about the military. I hadn't gone to a recruiter to talk about it, but it was always in the back of my mind as a backup plan. And this is before the Iraq, Afghanistan wars started. It was always something in the back of mind: if things go wrong, and I'm homeless, I can always count on the military to help. But instead of going to the military, I decided to move to Spain at the time and try a different life.

I moved to Spain and travelled around Europe, and within a year I came back. And then my nightmare became a reality. I ended up being homeless, without a place to stay. And then that was probably the first step when I started to talk to a recruiter, to the Marine Corps recruiter, about going into the military.

Normally how the recruitment works is usually in the neighbourhood where it's not pleasant. It was in Harlem, 125th Street. When you look around you, there's all kinds of social ills, and there's always a recruiting place where they have the Marine Corps, the army, the navy, the Coast Guard. You have abandoned streets. You have an abundance of people who were willing to come in and look for career opportunities. Unfortunately, I was one of those persons to look for something to better my life. Or so I thought.

My mother comes from a family of three brothers. Out of the three brothers, two were drafted. One was drafted in World War II. He suffered from post-traumatic stress and came back from the war. He drank heavily until he eventually died from alcoholism. The second one got drafted into the Korean War. It wasn't so much a patriotic thing. It was more that they got drafted, and at that time there was just no choice. The third one was about to get drafted too, for the Korean War. But he said something ridiculous, and they exonerated him from even entering the war.

So I had an idea about the military on some level. We didn't really talk so much about the trauma of war. It seemed like no one really did. They avoided talking about why my first uncle died of post-traumatic stress. This wasn't the conversation. The conversation was that he just drank himself to death, but not really coming to the conclusions that he'd experienced so many different traumatic things related to war: from what he saw in Germany and coming back. The drinking became an outlet and a comfort.

For me, going into the military was a financial decision, primarily. It also was stability, because I hadn't had much stability growing up: losing my parents, not having secondary family, really, to support me. So I was looking at it as going into a career as a soldier. In some ways I was being naive, although aware of some of the consequences that happened to my own family. But I took the risk. So I did go into the Marine Corps office and did the battery of tests that they have you do.

During this time, the war in Iraq had started. So I was already aware of that. But I knew that I didn't want to be infantry. I wanted to distance myself from that aspect of the war. So I tried to choose my job based on that. The job that I chose was to be working with helicopters, hopefully removed from the war zone. With recruiters, there was a conversation: if you choose helicopters, the likelihood of you going to Iraq is very small. You wouldn't be doing things that infantry guys would be doing. You've got to keep the aircraft safe. You can't have them in the middle of the war zone per se. So this is the way that they painted it for me.

And they talked about the type of life I would live. Of course, they talked about the girls and, you know, that was always a selling point. They talked about how physically fit you would be. They talked about how they'd take away your student loans, which was a huge bonus for me. They talked about after my service, I could go back to school and pursue my doctorate, which has always been the goal. So they painted the picture that things would be a lot better for me financially, and I would have the stability that I was looking for.

There were two points in my life when I was homeless: one before the Marine Corps and one before I joined the army. When I came back from Spain, I didn't have a place to stay. I stayed with a friend, so I never had a home. It's easiest staying with friends. I hadn't progressed to staying in homeless shelters yet.

There was a time when I stayed in a homeless shelter and I had to make a decision whether or not to go to another recruiter, or to go back into service, to stay out of a homeless shelter.

» When I decided to enlist in the Marine Corps, I was willing to give up my apartment in New York. I was willing to pretty much sacrifice my life, in a sense of all the things, the job and my apartment, to have greater stability and be in a far better situation. So I said, "All right." I quit my job, told my roommate I'm not coming back. Then I went into the Marine Corps. And, maybe within a couple of weeks, I was kicked out of the Marine Corps and ended up homeless.

Going into Marine Corps, you have your preconceived notions about what it's like. TV, films, and watching documentaries pretty much were on par with the expectations. But one thing that I didn't expect that threw a curveball at me was that they were going to single me out to be in charge of a platoon of soldiers. And they told me, whatever you do, stick your face down and just follow orders and don't say anything. Stay off the radar.

But because of my education and probably, you know, my physical background, they immediately saw me as a leader, and I was like, you can't say no. Right? So then, from that point on, the other soldiers look up to you, the recruits, they know they look up to you. And the curveball was, I've learned that many people who join the armed forces are coming from precarious backgrounds. I'm not saying all, but there's many people coming from broken homes, coming from broken situations. Some have some severe psychological issues. Just a whole variety. There was a discussion about whether people jumped from the frying pan right into the fire. This is what's happening.

One day a Marine recruit came up to me and said, "I can't take this, I want to kill myself or get out of this because this is just way too much. The stress is way too much." Which I understood. Because they don't, you know, the way they try to break you down is that you're small and you have little value. That's how hard this is structured. Being a social worker, when someone wants to kill themself, what am I supposed to do with this? Keep it to myself and don't report it or do I report it?

There is a duty to report, as a social worker and among people who work in social services, when someone who is in distress wants to either harm themselves or harm someone else. You have to report it to someone who's in charge to get the person who's in distress help. And I feel as though that was my duty—as a human being first, social worker second—just as a decent human being, to get this person help. I can't sit there and watch this person suffer extreme pain because of this institution.

When I reported it, it didn't go well with drill instructors in charge. For some reason they belittled him. And then I got in between the sergeant and him, and that created what you call a mutiny within the structure of military hierarchy.

The word was getting around to all the drill instructors that I was a troublemaker. I was just standing up for someone who was in need. He was in distress. And that threw me a curveball. So they started targeting me, and I didn't want this attention.

I wasn't accepting the abuse from the Marine Corps. And I don't care who it is. I mean, I didn't sign up to lose my job. I quit my job. All the things I gave up in my civilian life to just get beat up and abused in the system? No way. They weren't going to do that to me. So then they, of course, labelled me. And then they kicked me out of the Marine Corps. And that's when I became homeless. They gave me a bus ticket back to New York, and I had nothing to go back to but sleep on my friends' couches. And that set the stage for me going into the army.

I went back to New York. This was the second spell of being homeless. Right after college, I became homeless when I graduated. I stayed with a friend, but that relationship became strained. Not so much my friend, but it was just family dynamics, and I didn't have a place to stay. So I was staying in hotels on my days off. I would either sleep at work, or I was sleeping in hotels in New York. So that was the first spell of homelessness I ever experienced. And then the second spell of homelessness was when I got discharged from the Marine Corps. Then I had to live with friends again. That was really daunting. I would say I spent at least two years before I decided that it was time for me to go into the army. You know, sleeping on different people's couches, on the floors. This is just so much instability until one day I said, you know, I just had enough of this, and I went in to an army recruiter. I told him my situation. And he looked at my discharge from the Marine Corps. He said, "Well, you can join the army." And I said, "Well, do you have helicopters?" And he said, "Well, we have helicopters, and in the army you're gonna be guaranteed your job." And I said, "Okay. You know, I won't be doing infantry or any kind of combat-related job." And he said, "No." So I was really eager to sign because it was either going to a homeless shelter or going into the army.

Basically those were the choices that I had at the time. People would say, "Well, why don't you get a job?" But when you just have a bachelor's in social work or psychology, it is very, very competitive to get a job, because everyone has that. And then the jobs you get are so underpaid. So that became a very, very hard challenge. So, again, the army offers the same benefits: paying off my student debt, getting to go back to school, and if you decide you want to have a family, they would even pay for their school. So I'm thinking, I'm getting older, and if I decide to have a family, then they would be dependents. You even get extra money for having dependents. And they get shipped around wherever you go. This was a better lifestyle than the Marine Corps could offer.

Enlisting was financial support, livelihood, but also stability.

When I went into the army, I definitely learned from my mistakes in the Marine Corps. I stayed off the radar. I made it through boot camp without any issues. Then I went to AIT [advanced infantry training] for training with the helicopters. When I arrived there, off the bat, they're showing me that already the Iraq War, the second surge was in full swing. So they needed people. And they weren't training us to do helicopters. They were training us to do convoy protections and housing raids. And I'm putting two and two together, thinking, This is supposed to be happening at an infantry base, not at a helicopter base. And someone said, "This is exactly what you're going to be doing." I did not sign up for this. The recruiter basically lied to me, saying that, you know, the jobs that I get would be doing helicopters. I didn't want to be doing housing raids. I didn't want to do convoy protection because I know exactly what that means. You're gonna be pulling someone out in the middle of the night. You're going to be putting yourself at risk for IEDs [improvised explosive devices]. All the different horrors of war, it was going to be a reality for me.

People often ask, how can you be a social worker and be a soldier at the same time? And I struggle with that. You know, in order for me to live in my society, the trade-off is that I had to go into another society and kill somebody and maim them. I had to put them out of their home for me to have my own house. And I just thought about that. I said, "This doesn't make any sense." If people really thought about it like that, then I think people will have a second guess about joining the military. When you are a social worker, you always think about the social implications of your behaviour, and the social implications of society. And I thought about it. That helped push me to come to Canada, when I made a decision that it was time for me to leave. I thought, I can't do this. Ethically, it was definitely the wrong decision.

I knew that I had to get out, and I recalled from my studies, I read of the Vietnam draft dodgers and war resisters and that whole movement, that many of the resisters fled to Canada. I said to myself, Let me see about any war resisters fleeing to Canada. Are they having a kind of anti-war movement? I went to the library on the base, and I came across an anti-war campaign that was helping soldiers get out of the armed services of the United States and try to make a go at it in Canada. So I contacted them.

When I first came across the war resisters's website, I made a couple telephone calls and I didn't get through to anyone, but then eventually I was able to get through to Lee. And that made all the difference.

I remember it was Lee. Lee was the first person I contacted. I told him the situation and he said, "Hey, come get on the bus." Lee told me to come up to Canada and get on a bus from New York. I was in Virginia. So I came from Virginia to New York. He said, "Get on a bus from Penn Station and take the bus to Buffalo, and if you make it to the border, meet me at Toronto, the downtown station." Once I got to the border, there he was, right outside of the bus, waiting for me. I would say it was about a week between the time I spoke with Lee and boarded the bus.

And he, right off the bat, was like, "Hey, you're from New York?" I'm like, "Yeah." And he said, "I can tell by the accent. I'm from New York too." We connected immediately. He has such a warm personality. I just told him the situation and he's like, "Hey, you know, once you come to Canada, you know, we could provide a place and get you started," and he talked me through the process.

At the time, I was just so overwhelmed. I was just like, "I need an out," and not really hearing a lot of other options, only the hardships that I would face.

Initially, I was scared. But after talking to Lee, he kind of calmed my fears. At least someone was gonna be waiting for me on the other side. You see the pictures on the bus as it goes by and your bag is there and a whisk of dust goes by you and you're in the middle of nowhere. But Lee was there right at the bus door waiting for me. And I said, "Hey, so you must be Lee." And he said, "Yes." And I said, "I'm Linjamin." I put my hand out and then said, "Nice to meet you." And I think he gave me a hug, you know. And he said, "Welcome to Canada." It felt amazing to have somebody there waiting for you at the end of a long bus ride from Virginia to Toronto, potentially starting a new life, and to see the world from a different perspective. And then to have a connection for life, it was really a nice feeling.

Lee still had a definite New York accent. He welcomed me with open arms, and I think maybe even a hug. He tried to give me the Canadian rundown and his whole life of Canadianism within 15 minutes. The first place I remember him taking me was to Tim Hortons, and he said, "This is going to be a staple of Canadianism." He was a great guy. We remained friends 'til he died.[1]

» There are many people who are in the armed services that don't have a voice and can't speak out about the abuses that transpire within the armed services. Not only have I seen people try to commit suicide, I've seen sergeants and officers and even your own mates, comrades, be abusive. This goes on on a daily basis, and I have never seen this addressed. Ever. There were many attempts of me being compromised in that way, of being abused, and the daily restructuring of your whole persona of being in the military, which they do to break you down. But beyond that there was unbridled abuse, and I experienced that.

One of the things that people don't really talk about, or many people don't have a voice or do not mention, is the abuse that goes on within the military of the unsung people that are voiceless. I've seen it because someone spoke to me, and I've seen first-hand where people jumped from the frying pan into the fire. People try to commit suicide to get out because whatever stresses they're put under are totally amplified by going into the military. And my own personal experience in the army is there's more abuses that go on that are above and beyond just the everyday training that's supposed to go on. This creates a lot of discord in the military. Many people don't really talk about this, and it's important that this really gets out. It pushes people. People not only have post-traumatic stress from the war, but they have post-traumatic stress from the platoon. They have post-traumatic stress from the command that they're under. The brigade. Whatever entity under the military, there's that kind of post-traumatic stress in this, and that's not talked about or talked about very little.

Talk of mental health is looked at as if you're weak. People just didn't have an understanding of it. You're supposed to serve your country, but then your country is abusing you. How can anyone really deal with that? How can you go to war, and you're dealing with these problems? How can you go to war, seeing the atrocities of war, and you come back to your command, and then they're abusing you? That's two things at the same time. How can a person really handle that? That's not really talked about.

---

1. Lee, whose story appears in this book, died in 2024.

If it was me, I think the army should be happy that people are serving. They should do everything to make sure that the soldiers are comfortable, not make them uncomfortable.

And I said, I'm gonna go into Iraq, Afghanistan, killing people, just to have a life in the United States? But I'm definitely not gonna lose my life. Also, I'm getting screwed over, getting abused by a system and people that I'm supposed to have some kind of allegiance to? I say no way. I was through with it. My decision was solidified. I wiped my hands of it. And I said I was gonna go to Canada.

And I knew the consequences. The consequences were if within 30 days you don't show up for formation, they send out a federal arrest warrant. And I was willing to take that chance. I wasn't looking back.

» I'd never been to Canada before. I knew that it touched New York State. I knew I always wanted to go to Montreal; Quebec was the Europe of North America. When I looked up war resisters, I initially wanted to go to Montreal before Toronto because I wanted the European vibe. But the fact that I didn't speak French, I thought that there could be a serious dilemma trying to find work. So I opted to go to Toronto and see what that was like. And it was very different to what I had imagined.

I initially thought, It's no more than an hour and a half from Buffalo, so it couldn't be that much more different than the United States. But it was really, really different. People were very different. What people talk about is very different. Even the word "about" is different. People talk about "eh." They'd say "eh" as affirmations. The politics were different. The parliamentary system was very different from our system of government. Just very, very different. On the surface it may seem American because the accent is not that far off, but it's really a world away.

For the most part, I was welcomed with open arms. But working-wise, I felt it a little bit difficult at the very beginning, because they wanted Canadian experience. I ran into a lot of barriers there. Being a social worker in New York doesn't transfer to being a social worker in Canada or in Toronto. It's because people aren't as direct as they are in New York. You run into a lot of different cultural risks and differences that I had to learn to adapt to. But once I got the hang of it, things really opened up. And I stayed in Toronto for eight years.

When I first came to Canada, within the first week, I had to make a refugee claim. You can either make the claim at the border—but that can get a little bit dicey, because they can send you right back. Or you can make a refugee claim within Canada. Right when it was the weekend, I made a refugee claim inside of Canada.

You never think that you can be a refugee from your country. Everyone thinks that America's the best. First off, you're never going to get refugee status, because America's supposed to be free and has a democratic process, etc. I was hopeful at one point. Then I wasn't hopeful at the same time, because I knew that the likelihood of Canada admitting soldiers to come in would be a political nightmare. It would open up a portal for many more soldiers from the United States to come here. So I knew that it was a slim opportunity that I would get status.

My refugee claim went through the process pretty quickly, probably within a year of getting into Canada, a year and a half. But it just didn't hold any weight, because they were just deporting people. It lasted for about a year and a half, and then it just looked dark. I then talked to a lawyer who was able to help me find a way where I could stay in Canada under the NAFTA [North American Free Trade Agreement] agreement. My refugee claim was eventually denied. But then I stayed on as a NAFTA worker in Toronto.

I first stayed in London [Ontario] while I waited on my refugee claim to be processed. There were certain people who you stay with, host homes that were set up in Toronto or different places. I met a lovely lady who was part of the war resister campaign and said that they were going to start a chapter in London. I became one of the first war resister refugees in London. She and her family welcomed me into their home for about three or four months until I got my work visa.

At the time, it was tough, living in London. It was a nice city. And I met some really, really nice people. But it was tough because that's when I first came and getting to know Canada. I didn't have access to a car yet because I didn't have any money. So my life was very, very limited. And then that put a lot of strain on me. You start questioning, What are you doing here and why are you here? Was it a good decision? In the meantime, waiting every day, looking in the mail, when is that work visa coming? Then, finally, it came, and I was like, yes!

I then got a telephone call from Lee saying that a person who's loosely affiliated with war resisters knows someone who has a basement apartment in Toronto. And you're more than welcome to come look at it and meet her and stay. And that was it. I moved to Toronto.

My life in Toronto started out with basically nothing, from zero. Socially, my life started to grow. I met more people, started to get out more. I started going to the gym. Fitness has always been a big part of it for me. So I met people at the gym. They would recognize my face, and that created a sense of community. And, of course, I would go to some of the war resisters' meetings. I had my little cafes that I would go to, my bakeries that I'd visit. Some of the families who were interested in the stories would invite me out to go to their homes or dinner to meet their family. So socially, it is probably the most stable it has ever been in my whole life.

Finding work, probably for the first six months, was daunting, because I didn't have the Canadian experience. I got my first job in Brampton. But with no car, it was like a two-hour train. But it gave me that Canadian experience, and I did what I had to do. I worked in schools and then that evolved to working in the school districts, the Toronto District School Board. I worked in group homes with various social service agencies within Toronto. It was a really good experience, where I met a lot of people.

Plus, I lived downtown. So, you know, enjoying the nightlife.

But sometimes good things come to an end.

Unfortunately, because I was just a NAFTA worker, my job was dependent on my work permit. And with the economics of the time, I wasn't getting jobs. We were contractors. Contractors are competitive with other contractors, and they got outbid for a lot of jobs, like at SickKids hospital. I was working at SickKids hospital for quite some time. And they got outbid by another contractor who paid their workers a lot less. SickKids, unfortunately, took those contracts and basically put me out of work. So I had to look for something else.

When you have bills, and then, again, the stability factor comes in. I knew the key to my stability was to get more higher education than I had. I wanted to become a registered nurse. And I knew that if I stayed in Canada, it was going to be hard because I wasn't a resident and I'd have to pay international fees. So I had to come back to the United States to go back to school.

» When I came back to the United States, it was reverse culture shock. When you stay in a place for eight years, you don't realize how the place grows on you, becomes home. When you move around and you see a lot of the world, your alliances shift. And my alliances have shifted. When I first came home, one of the first things that I recognized, off the bat, was how dense the racism, the segregation. Immediately, I could see that, when I started living back in the home society.

The conversations, things that people talk about, were very, very different. When I talk, I never really say I'm leftist or conservative or this or that. But those conversations are just not even happening, or maybe they're starting to happen now. But they weren't happening here. You know, when you say "universal health care," that's like a nasty word here. People were okay paying these high premiums for private care. When I tell people that I had universal health care and could go see a doctor as many times as I want and I would never see a bill, they had no understanding of that. Those things have shifted in my life. It was very, very difficult. And even five years later, I still had reverse culture shock.

I still haven't adapted. How can you adapt? Things change no matter where you go. Things are always in motion, whether you're in one country versus the other country. But the way that people think about things in the other country are entirely different: people's outlook.

Now, years on, it is still very difficult. I've been swinging from state to state, from California to Arizona. Some things have worked, and some things haven't. I'm still trying to find that stability. Peace is still very elusive. Still, I'm aspiring to be an RN.

Being a person of colour in Canada versus being a person of colour in the United States plays out very, very differently across the border. It started with me growing up in the United States before coming to Canada: you become accustomed to segregated neighbourhoods, social inequality, to these different social ills plaguing American society. I can never change my skin colour or my background. But I can transplant myself to another country.

Going to Canada as a Black person—I'm not saying that racism doesn't exist in Canada, because it does, and you see it. But it's not as dense as it is in the United States. What I mean by that is, it was the first time where I can go to a multicultural, suburban neighbourhood that would have whites, Sikhs, Indians, Black people or people from Caribbean descent, European descent—just really diverse, people's background. The first time I was seeing this, I was really astounded. I was like, wow, this place is really transforming what multiculturalism is all about. I didn't have to really be scared someone's gonna judge you because of your skin colour: the point where I've become an individual first before my skin colour. While here [the US] is the opposite: skin colour first, then you become an individual.

When I lived in various places in Toronto, my building would be multicultural. I never felt that because you had a certain skin colour you couldn't live here. *I felt that I was wanted.* While in the US, you can feel whether or not you're wanted right away. You can feel those disparities. You feel the disconnect. So that's one of the issues that I struggle with living here, and one of the differences between Canada and the United States.

Another difference in terms of race and racism that I saw in Canada versus the United States is the social groups and the social constructs. I had the privilege of working at the Toronto school board and seeing how the narratives are different in the literature that the children receive. When the kids are reading their literature, they're seeing the Asian person, a Black person, the person that has a disability. They're all learning to cohabitate. Whereas in some of the literature here in the United States, that's not occurring. And that's why you are still seeing the disconnect that's still prevalent in the United States society today.

Another example that's very different, too, is the disconnect between the person and people in the government. What I mean is, not only in local government, but also their federal government. I had a situation where I needed to come back into Canada. After my refugee claim was denied, I left voluntarily. They wouldn't allow me to come back on my NAFTA papers. What I learned through the War Resisters Support Campaign is how they petition the federal government, and I got to know the Members of Parliament (MPs). So I said to myself, Okay, well, maybe I should call my MP, telling her the difficulties I'm having with my NAFTA papers. Maybe she could call the Canadian consul in New York and see if they can help me out. And guess what? Within a week, something that could've taken months to resolve, was resolved in a matter of days. I think people

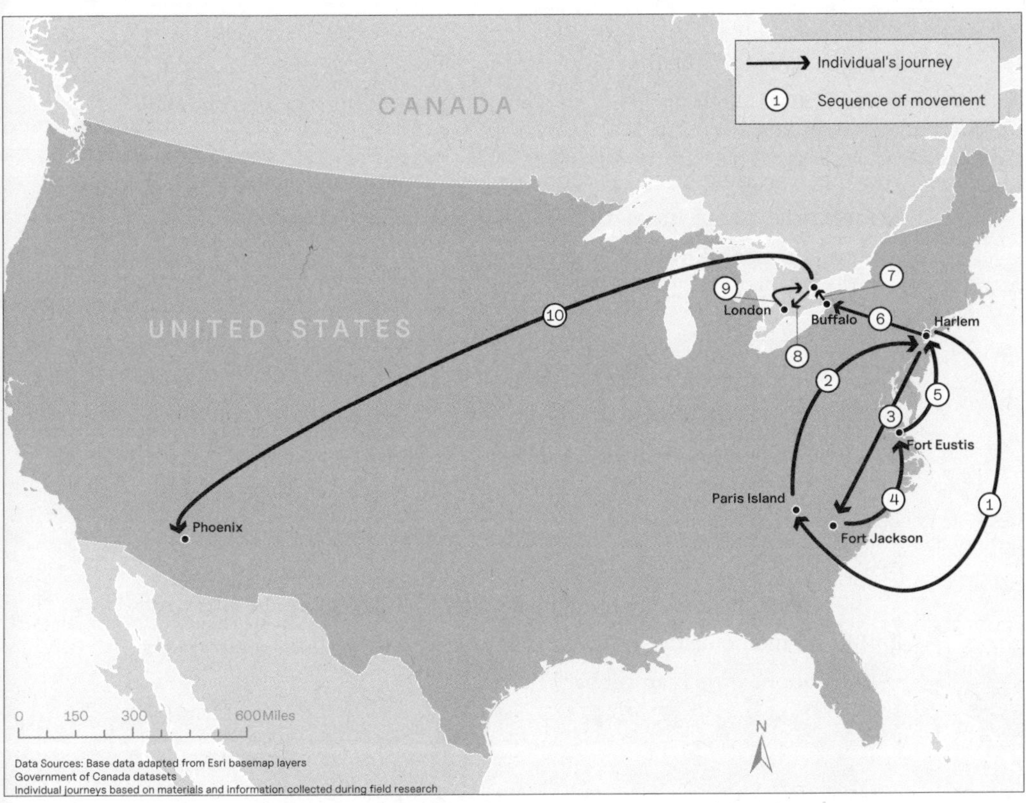

MAP 3: Linjamin's journey from the United States to Toronto and then London, Ontario, in 2004, and his return to the United States in Phoenix, Arizona, seven years later.

in Canada have more of a connection with people in the federal government than people in the United States have with their federal government, which was a big difference. I feel that we are just totally disconnected from our senators and our members of Congress.

» People ask me, "Where's home? Where would you go? Where would you be with your many different experiences in different countries?" I've said many times that I'd love to go back to Canada, to relive some of my experiences. I definitely had a good time there. I have no negative feelings or any negativity that prevents me from wanting to go back to Canada. It has always been positive; I've had positive experiences with many different people and many different laughs. People ask me, "What is it like living in Canada?" The first thing that happens to me: my face will light up and I start laughing. Being 30-something and living in a metropolitan area, being a young person, being free and able to gain life experiences was very liberating for me. It definitely elevated my mind. Being able to meet many people from diverse backgrounds pushed me to be more accepting of people from all backgrounds.

I know in the United States I have no alliances to anywhere. The United States is not my home. It's just my place I was born, what I got indoctrinated into. Toronto was somewhat by choice or by opportunity. But then I came back as a NAFTA worker by choice. So that became an adopted country. So that was by choice. United States wasn't by choice.

Canada and the United States are vastly different places. There are positives and negatives about both. But I do have my preferences. I do prefer living in Canada versus the United States.

Is Toronto my home? is a tough question. That's where your alliances lie. But I could honestly say Toronto's home now in my heart. I always try to think about ways I can get back there.

Soldiers running. (Photo courtesy of Nuk213/Shutterstock.com. Used with permission.)

6 Neil

MY CONSCIOUS HISTORY of this period comes when I was in university in St. Louis—Washington University. We had lived all over the United States, and we were raised in a very progressive home. Vietnam was raging by the time I was ready to graduate in '68. I didn't graduate until '69, but by that time there were all kinds of demonstrations against the war.

I was against the war in Vietnam from the word go. During university I was a draft counsellor. I knew options to evade at that time. Still, I went into the army immediately after graduating. I didn't want to leave my country, but I knew I wouldn't fight in Vietnam. I also knew that I didn't want to go to jail. As I look back on it, I think, How convoluted. I knew I was against the war in Vietnam, I knew I'd never fight there, but I wanted the specific experience of the military because I didn't want to leave my homeland. I also didn't want to go to jail. Therefore, I had to accept, initially, to be drafted. I wanted to see what I was going to get assigned.

Not only that. When I think back on it, I just can't believe that I didn't check the box. At that time, if you were gay and you checked the box, you were automatically disqualified from the military. By that time I knew that I was gay, but I guess I wasn't ready: I didn't want to admit it. I definitely didn't want to admit it on a document. I have to say that these things are very difficult to understand about yourself.

Looking back on it as a pensioner now, I can't understand why I didn't take this one option that I could have taken and saved so much trouble and stress. But I didn't. That is all there is to it. So I have to say now, 50 years later, that I wasn't out. I knew that I was gay, but I guess I was wavering because I had had experience both ways. I didn't check the box. Now you can't check the box, there is no box to check. Not only that, but I can look back on it, and I'm going on in detail because this amazes me, that this is the way that I acted at that time with a college degree.

The other thing was, I went to a recruiter, and he told me, "Oh yeah, you could, with a college degree, choose your MOS [military occupational specialty]." And I believed him! This guy, these people, lied through their teeth about what the military was going to do. They get commissions for every recruit that they sign up.

So, big mistake: I joined the military. I enlisted in March of 1969. I was four months in the military, and I crossed the border in August. I had my physical, went in, had my basic training. I took it at Fort Leonard Wood in Missouri. That's two months, basic. I liked basic because I liked getting in shape. It was mostly physical training, and I tried to ignore the psychological stuff: the racism and hatred that they try and brainwash you with. It was hard to take. They try and psychologically cut you down so you have no personal volition, and you follow orders and all this stuff.

But there are some things that I will never forget that I saw in basic training. One, in particular, I will never forget. They had us march over a fat guy. And it was just sickening to watch my platoon, some of the guys who stepped on him, kicked him. Most people did not do this, I don't think, but I can remember them doing this, and I was just disgusted. He was in the army. He was in our platoon. There's always somebody that they pick out to denigrate and make fun of, to make themselves feel bigger.

The other thing that made me sick was our bayonet training. You're out there, and you have to yell at the top of your voice, "Kill! Kill!" And you're stabbing this dummy and all this kind of stuff that went against my beliefs totally. But it was stuff that I can slough off. So I did well in basic training.

It just never ended, the corruption and degradation that happened. I remember I bribed a guy to give me a high score on my marksmanship test at the end of basic training. I paid him something, which is another thing that goes against my principles. But I guess you have no principles when you're trying to get through and keep your head down, remain anonymous, not provoking them.

All the other guys that were in my company were like kids to me. Here I was with a college degree, and almost everybody there was barely out of high school, if that. I didn't have much respect for them. They all had huge Southern accents and were ignorant, basically. Maybe more like they acted ignorantly. I didn't have any friends that I can remember. I had a few friends in university that came out to visit me. I really was thankful for that. I thought that was a beautiful gesture.

So at the end of two months, I pass. I go on to the army after basic, to advanced infantry training. By then I probably knew that I wasn't going to get what I chose. I was assigned to be a radio operator at Fort Knox, Kentucky. By that time it was summertime, and Fort Knox, Kentucky, is hot as hell. The little sadistic things that the army makes you do: we had to wear our army shirt, which was heavy cotton, buttoned up at the neck, and the arms are long-sleeved, buttoned-up. They did that to make you a little more miserable and break you down a little more.

Here is another segment of my story that when I look back on it, I just do not understand: how I could not learn the Morse code. Here I was with a college degree, and we worked in a lab practising Morse code for at least four to six hours a day. And I couldn't learn the Morse code. As I look back on it, I must have unconsciously decided at that time not to cooperate with the military. One: because a radio operator could be one of the most vulnerable people in the platoon in Vietnam. The antenna of the radio that the operator carries on his back is the first target in a firefight, because that's the communication with the battalion. So people were telling me, "Oh, you could be assigned to a colonel here, stateside, driving his Jeep around, or you could be the first one shot in Vietnam." Now in the army, if you are not able to do what they tell you to do, you fail in the course, and then they give you one more chance. I had another chance, one more month, or something, of this training, and I still wasn't able to learn the Morse code. They reassign you after your second chance if you don't succeed.

Psychologically, this is incredible to me. I got a terrible assignment that I knew was going to lead directly to Vietnam. I had intellectually prepared myself and understood where I stood in regards to Vietnam. I knew I would never fight or accept this assignment.

During the time that I was at Fort Knox, it was hotter than hell, and we would have to wait in line. It was like torture to get lunch, with horrible food the cooks were sweating in and spitting in and who knows what else. Everybody was in a bad mood. So I decided, rather than eat lunch and wait and go through this hell, I was going to skip it. I was going to go to a VA [Veterans Affairs] hospital to eat.

I found the huge cafeteria in the basement of the tower and started eating lunch over there. During that time I met a guy that had been to Vietnam and was finishing up his tour. At that time, we had two years: one year active duty and then the next year, the second year, in the States. So he was back in the States. I will never forget making his acquaintance and saying, "Tell me, what did you go through over there? Tell me your experience over there." He very quietly and calmly told me about his horror. That was pretty important in my journey. He was a good guy too. He wasn't excited, he wasn't loud, he just calmly told me about the hell he went through. He had PTSD as far as I could tell, probably from this experience. I knew intellectually that I wouldn't leave my country, but psychologically I wasn't quite prepared to go to Canada. After that experience, I sat there speechless about the horrors he went through. And I knew, I don't care what they do to me, I will never do this. I will never get within spitting distance of this war.

They did reassign me, to reconnaissance. There's no chance that I'm going to be in the States with reconnaissance, you know, in search of the enemy. So I go, "That's it, now I know what I am going to do."

My plan was to go back home, get my stuff, and get North. I had a younger friend in the military at that time, and we were both planning to go to Canada. He turned out to be not as serious as I was, and he kept saying, "Oh, I'm not ready to go. Let's not do this right now, not this week." He kept putting it off. I go, "Okay, that's fine. I'm going to go. I'm not waiting anymore."

Unfortunately, he must have been very immature because word got around. I obviously told him, "I don't want you to say anything about this," and somebody then, before I left, said, "Okay, Neil, when are you going?" I didn't want them to know this; I didn't want word to get out. But, you know, guys talk about things. Anyway. I said, you know, "None of your business."

Military forts are like cities. Fort Knox is gigantic. It has a bus terminal, a shopping centre. It has everything. Guys were coming and going all the time with passes. So my plan was to get on the bus and go into Louisville and get a bus south to Knoxville. Knoxville was the city where I would change to a smaller bus to Oak Ridge, where my family lived.

I got my clothes and my boots and packed them in a laundry bag. I didn't think about what this would look like until I got into the lineup for the bus in the morning. I didn't realize, but one of those boots was showing a sharp angle. I was really nervous, as you can imagine. MPs [military police] would patrol the bus terminal, walk up and down. My plan was, if they asked me, to tell them that I was going to do my laundry in Louisville. There were laundry facilities on the base, but that was my plan. I was not pushing ahead in line, but it was going so slow. The bus driver is checking the tickets. You have to have a pass to get off the base, so I was illegal from the start. But I just couldn't get the idea of this angle showing in my duffel. This really freaked me out, and I was just thinking, "Go! Go ahead! Please!" I finally got to the bus driver, and he's checking my ticket and then, boom, I'm bounding up the steps, and those guys—the MPs—just passed me right at the time.

» Before I had left for basic, my father took me up in a private plane to look at the topography of east Tennessee, of my homeland, which is so beautiful. It was a sweet thing that he did, and he said, "I'm proud of you" when we came back. I said, "I'm not proud of myself."

But Dad was more conservative than I thought when I was growing up. You look up to your parents, growing up. I loved my parents. My father and I, in my university years, were separated. We started separating then. I remember the Democratic National Convention was in Chicago. I was just furious about the riots there. I was pretty radical, and Dad thought that I was going too far. Basically, he asked me to leave. He said, "If you don't have respect for us, you know, you're going to have to leave the house." So we did have our separation there, but then it never came to that, it never went that far. But I know that he moved to the right very much in his older years. We didn't have political discussions with my mother. And I was closer to my mother than my father. So I never had a strong disagreement at that time with my mother. I adored my mother right to the end.

I have to say that they supported whatever I did, but they weren't enthusiastic. Later, with my life in Canada, they became much more supportive. They were always supportive of me and their other children. I have three sisters. I'm the oldest, and we're close in age. And they were always supportive of me, but not until a few years later.

I have a lot of respect for my father, and I forgive him for his distance and coolness towards me. I was hurt by this. When I moved to Canada, I was basically on my own. He didn't support me. I supported myself. He never asked me about my life, and this hurt. And then many years later, my eldest sister, who's a year and a half younger than myself, told me, "Every time that I see Dad, he asks me about you, how your life is." I go, "I'm so glad you told me that. Because I didn't think he gave a damn about my life."

These things were very strong in those years, tore all kinds of families apart. And me, relatively speaking, I was lucky. I was lucky with my parents, and I was lucky with my journey. Very lucky.

» So I made it. I got to Oak Ridge at 5:30 in the morning. I walked home at 5:30 in the morning from the bus terminal, and walked up the hill to my boyhood house and knocked on the door. My whole life my mother would get up at 5:30, before anyone else in the family. This was her time to read and have her coffee and think about her day. And so she was up, and she opened the door and said, "Well, is this what I think it is?" And I said, "Yeah, Mom." She goes, "Okay, come on in hon, have some breakfast." I can just see her there, standing at the door and welcoming me. Yup, that was a beautiful thing.

I knew enough that they weren't going to come after me. They don't come after people that are AWOL immediately. There are thousands of AWOLS. So I had plenty of time to pack, say my goodbyes and be with my family, and make my leisurely way north.

My mother kept saying, "When are you going to leave?" She was very nervous. I go, "Mom, they aren't coming after me like that. Don't worry." Anyway, she just basically shoved me out of the house very quickly. She kept encouraging me to leave and get my stuff together.

One thing that I knew was happening was here on the west coast crossings to Vancouver, deserters were being sent back. This was routine. Border officials were asking men what their military status was when they were presenting themselves at the border. And if they were in the military, they were sent back. If they were draft dodgers, they were let across. The thing that was a miracle at that time, [Pierre] Trudeau was the prime minister, and two weeks before I crossed at the Rainbow Bridge in Niagara Falls, Trudeau directed the immigration officials, saying, "Their military status is not relevant at the border."

I could have very easily been one of those men that they turned back, two weeks before me. But because Trudeau sent this direct order to the customs authorities, they stopped asking this question. Two weeks before I crossed!

I found that out later through the draft counselling, the support of Americans and Canadians in Canada. That was a tremendous network at that time. We do not have anything like that now for war resisters. The Vietnam War was hated by Canadians and Americans to such an extent that Iraq doesn't compare to it. Although Iraq is pretty much hated too. And Syria. And all the wars that have happened after. But I was tremendously blessed with support every step of the way. Amazing! When I look back on it, I just cannot believe how lucky I was.

It is so difficult to be an immigrant. I had never set foot in Canada before in my life. I was 25 at the time, not as young as some of these war resisters, but I was still young. I did not want to leave my homeland; I loved my homeland.

It was hard getting established. I had very little job experience, even with a college degree. A BA is not worth very much, as people find out. The job situation was very difficult.

I had some hard times. Not only that, but I came out in Canada at that time. I came out, and I started going out and meeting people. It was pretty grim back in those days; bars were pretty grim. But I'll never forget the Parkside, [a bar] downtown. There are famous bars in Toronto that are probably no longer there. But they were real dives. It was a sad time.

» I knew Niagara Falls was busy because it was August. I'll never forget when I crossed. And I want to say some things about that. I was very nervous. I was going to say "I'm crossing to visit." Who is going to believe this, looking into the back seat of my car filled up? They didn't even ask me to open the trunk. They said, "Okay, have a good stay, have a good visit in Canada." I said, "Thank you, sir!" My dear mother had packed me a picnic basket to last me for weeks.

The first thing I did was look at the falls when I stopped in a picnic place. I called my parents, and I go, "Good morning from Niagara Falls, Ontario!" It was so beautiful and such a relief. I had no idea what the future was going to bring, but I got across that line. I unpacked my mom's lunch, went to the water fountain, and talked to a Canadian couple that was there. I told them, "This is my first experience in Canada." She came back to my table with a Coke and said, "Welcome to Canada!" I thought, I'm going to like this place. I knew it would be a good country.

» I went to Toronto. Because I had been a draft counsellor in university, this is where my experiences helped, because I knew exactly where to go. I went to the Union of American Exiles house there. They were busy. At the time, maybe 20 or more men were crossing the border every day to immigrate to Canada. So this was a big thing. There were people coming into this house, requesting landed status, information. I walked into a living room where guys were relaxing. They had a desk and counsellors, and there were people making food. It was really busy, like a beehive.

I wanted to get landed as soon as possible. And they said, "Well, if you want that then you have to go to Ottawa." There were references there, Canadian families who were taking in US war resisters and letting them stay for a certain period of time. So I just went to Ottawa and got information, a place to stay. I stayed with a couple that lived on the Quebec side.

I applied for landed status in Hull, Quebec. At that time they had the point system. I passed: I was accepted as a landed immigrant. I got my landed status and a place to stay. I went back to Toronto, briefly, and got a job as a childcare worker, working with emotionally disturbed kids. It was a tough job that I didn't stay at long. Then I got a job with the medical plan in Ontario.

During that time my family had come to visit me. I'd gone through my first homesickness. I had decided, "Okay, I'm moving to Vancouver." I lived in a basement in Vancouver. I agreed to do handyman work and carpentry work on this mansion that I lived at.

I was working towards moving to the Gulf Islands. I ended up having a lot of part-time jobs, not very good jobs. Eventually, I go, "Oh, I'm going to get out of this place. I want to live on the Gulf Islands." And I had a boyfriend there too, for a little while.

First I went to Salt Spring Island, then on to Mayne Island. I had a place to live, I met a few people. I ended up staying there for 12 years with a small business: a trash business. It was 1972. I was renting a small cabin, living way below poverty level. But at that time you could. And I still, actually, live below poverty level.

It was hard to make a living over there—so we had to hustle. I took pottery, a course in Vancouver, all kinds of creative stuff that we did. It was a great life. We had to be very flexible. I was a jack of all trades: taught myself to learn how to use a chainsaw, lived on 60 acres of forest, thinned the forest, built a workshop with a lot of help from my friends. It was a great time.

I've always been a war resister and objected to our governments in the United States and Canada. I've always been, to a certain degree, an activist, involved in issues that I'm concerned with. I became a respectable member of the community. We had a small war resistance group over there. At that time the US Navy had a test area at Nanoose Bay on Vancouver Island. We were trying to close this military installation. They were testing torpedoes and stuff like this. They actually had military housing there. We were protesting the Vietnam War. We would have bake sales and thrift sales to support our group.

» I did one thing that was crucially important. I found out through the war resistance network in Canada that there was one fort in the United States that you could go to and get discharged, no matter how long you'd been gone. The Quakers are big proponents of this back east.

By that time the FBI had come to my mother's door and asked her about me. This was early in my life in Canada, in the '70s—and she told them, "We don't know where he is." They never came back. I only heard about this later. I was pretty mad. I hated to have them be involved in my situation like this, to be vulnerable in this way.

It turns out that at any time the base commander can discharge anybody, no matter how many years AWOL. I was probably classified in the army's documents as a deserter. At that time, it was seven years gone, from 1969 to 1976. I heard about this program. The base commander could discharge a deserter with an undesirable discharge—not a dishonourable discharge.

All this time, seven years, I didn't dare go across the border. My parents and sisters all came up to visit me. During that time, Dad flew them up in his small plane. We were not close politically, but we were still close, still a family. I love all my sisters, and they're all different and very unique. I wanted to be able to cross the border. The only thing was, I was very hesitant about this because I'd never heard of this program. Nobody's ever heard of it. You're taking a big chance. You could end up in the stockade by presenting yourself.

So I said to the counsellor, or the person I heard this from, I said, "Okay, I would like to talk to a person that's done this. Before I do this myself, I have to talk to a person who has done this." So I did, and he said, "Yes, this is true." So I promptly went back from the east coast. I crossed into New York illegally. I went to Port Authority and got a bus directly to Fort Dix, New Jersey. I turned myself in as soon as I got there. They started on the paperwork, and they assigned me to this particular company that was full of all of us, from all over, doing the same thing. I did get my discharge. My dad said, "Don't do this, you deserve more than an undesirable discharge." At the time it was Carter's administration, and Carter gave amnesty to draft dodgers, but not deserters. Big difference. As time would tell, I did the right thing. Who cares whether I got an undesirable discharge. The army was undesirable to me, too!

» One of the things that I feel so bad about is I want young war resisters now to have the chance that I had. This really breaks my heart: that men and women today do not have the chance to have a life in Canada like I did. I feel so bad about my brothers and sisters sent back now as resisters, as moral people, as humans having to go through a court martial and be sentenced. Some were lucky and had a few years; some have been unlucky. With the change of government, we protested and said, "We want those guys to be able to legally stay here." They already went through hearings and some have been accepted, but [Stephen] Harper put a stop to that. Justin Trudeau put off their hearings.

Pierre Trudeau is a hero of mine. His policies were independent of the United States. Of course, times have changed. Things are different, and the pressure is a lot worse now on countries, on Canada. Pierre Trudeau was a great and independent Canadian. He did many good things.

I still have tremendous affection for America. I am in strong disagreement with Canadian foreign policy and the Canadian government. Public policy is degraded. But the country, the people, and the land are magnificent. Of course, it's magnificent in the States. I would say I'm North American. I have no problem saying I'm Canadian and feeling glad and grateful that I get to live here. I don't have any nostalgia; I don't miss it. I have no intention of moving back.

John relaxing at the beach. (Photo courtesy of John.)

7 John S.

I WAS BORN NOVEMBER 11, 1947, ironically, on Remembrance Day, on Veteran's Day in the States. I grew up in a very solid kind of Midwestern family in a small suburb of St. Louis, Missouri.

I had a pretty conventional, middle-class upbringing. I was very independent. I had a thousand things that I was interested in. I played junior league baseball and was involved in athletics from childhood. I started my first two years of school in a racially segregated school system, which had some significance later. I went all the way through school there. I was the president of my student body in high school. I was the first chair violin in the orchestra. I was the co-quarterback of the only undefeated football team in the state. I ran track. I played tennis. I played basketball. I went to church and youth fellowship all the way through high school. It was a fairly conventional Midwestern life. I was very achievement oriented. I liked being successful at what I did.

When I was an adolescent, I would be Friday night going to a dance at the country club, and Saturday night hanging out down by the river, having a beer with the guys from the wrong side of the tracks. I never locked in on a social group. I know now that wasn't typical.

I was very close with my father. He travelled a lot. But when he was home, he put all three of us—my two sisters and me—he always was the one who put us to bed. It was a ritualized kind of thing: 10 or 15 minutes of alone time with Dad to talk about whatever was on your mind. He passed on his point of view on the world in a really direct way. Like, "This above all, to thine own self be true." That was his guiding light. He said, "I don't have to agree with you, but you do what you think is the right thing." Because, he said, "You've got to live with you. I don't have to live with you, but you do." He always, with all three of the kids, always pushed that: being honest with yourself, being who you really thought you were. I realized later that it made a big influence when the time came to make that decision about military service and what was going to be true for me.

The other two precepts he had were "Nothing but good could come to me and mine," and "Every day, in every way, I'm better and better." Those latter two precepts extended to everyone else. He was very clear: it wasn't because you were white, it wasn't because you were middle class, it wasn't because you lived in some country—that's everybody. Although he was not a conscientious objector, he served in World War II in the navy for two years, and completely disagreed with my letter when I filed for conscientious objection, he didn't back off from what he taught us as kids. "You know, if you think that's the right thing to do," he said. "Let me tell you, there will be consequences for this. Any big decision like this has consequences. But if that's the right thing that you gotta do, it's what you gotta do." When the time came, and I was making these decisions about what I wanted to do with the military as a late adolescent, though he didn't agree with me, he supported me. And that's been probably the greatest gift that anybody could give me.

I think in terms of music a lot. Music is a big part of my life. I had a pivotal moment, a seminal moment. It came in an instant. And I know exactly when it was and where I was and how it happened. I went to Georgetown University in Washington, DC. I graduated early. I was in college when I was 17. I had a deferment when I was 17, 18, 19, 20. So for the bulk of that time, I didn't even really think about it a whole lot. I was just going to college and studying hard and having a good time. I was also an athlete; I was in rowing, I was up and down the east coast, a pretty typical college student. However, I was in Washington, DC, and there was a lot of political activity there. The Students for a Democratic Society [activist] Tom Hayden spoke on campus a lot when I was there because they wanted to have a strong local college base so that when they did call demonstrations at the White House, or at the Capitol, or at the Pentagon, they could generate a significant number of people quickly. So they recruited hard there. Honestly, Georgetown is a pretty conservative place. It was mainly prep school boys and the few of us that came out of public school. So they didn't have a great audience for left-wing politics most of the time on Georgetown's campus in 1965. Largely, it was the sons of America's Catholic wealthy.

I was raised United Church of Christ, Evangelical and Reformed. It was one of those kinds of combination churches. You know, middle of the road. I did have a youth fellowship worker, however, that I had a close relationship with, and he was very involved in the ecumenical movement. He often presented to us the idea that there are many spiritual journeys, many paths forward, many of which are headed the same direction, it's just a different path. That did influence my decision later too.

There were two pivotal moments when I knew I had a big decision to make about military service. Number one: when I was either a junior or early in my senior year in college they had the deal where they drew all of the birthdays out of a barrel, and that gave you your number: the draft lottery. My number was 7. So that day, everybody sat around in the student union to watch, because if your birthday was drawn like number 10 or 20, you were pretty sure that as soon as your student deferment was gone, you were going to be drafted, you were going to have to go into the army whether you wanted to or not. If you got a number like, if they drew your birthday number 320, you could kind of go: "That's not a problem. I'm not going to get drafted." Because the chances that they are going to go up that high were unusual.

I had number seven. So I knew that when I graduated, I was going to have to deal with this. I couldn't avoid it. So I spent that last year at university in various modes of thinking. It wasn't completely clear at that point. At the same time, I submitted an application for Officer Candidate School. Particularly among upper-middle-class boys, there was a sense, "Well, if I gotta go, I may as well go as an officer and make more money and possibly be safer than hiking around in a rice paddy with people shooting over my head."

My thinking was not really settled in that last year. In June of 1969 I came out of college. My student deferment was over. But at that time, teachers, doctors, nurses were still deferred, seen as critical workers. In 1969 and '70, my first year of teaching, and in my second year of teaching, the beginning of the 1970 school year, I was still deferred because I was a teacher. But they were running out of bodies. At that point they sent, oh, I don't know what, 350,000 different people, I think, to Vietnam, and they were running out of people to draft. So they dropped all of those employment deferments. That's when it really hit the wall, when I knew, "Now, buddy. You've gotta decide, are you gonna go or are you not gonna go?"

This was the fall of 1970. That's when I had no other means of avoiding it. At that point, I was married. I didn't have any children yet. But I realized that I had already made the decision a long time before that. My seminal moment was the day after Robert Kennedy was shot. We went through a lot, you know, with John Kennedy being shot, [Martin Luther] King being shot, the [Eugene] McCarthy movement and that movement just dying, the anti-war movement with McCarthy that I worked on as a student in university. In that summer I stayed to go to Georgetown summer school, in June of '68, just before I graduated. I came home from class one night, and they went, "Robert Kennedy has been killed." As the third assassination in those five years, I was kind of numb at that point. I just went, "You know, I'm not surprised."

The next day I went to class in the morning, and I was walking back to my dormitory at noon, and somebody had a big window open, and out of this window I heard Buffy Sainte-Marie singing the song, "Universal Soldier." I had never heard the song before; somebody was just blasting it out of this window the morning after Robert Kennedy was shot. I remember stopping in the central part of Georgetown's campus, right in front of this dormitory, hearing her sing these lines: "He's the universal soldier, and he really is to blame."

Hearing those words and the rest of it, "His orders come from far away no more. They come from him, and you, and me, and brothers, can't you see? This is not the way we put an end to war." It just immediately connected with everything that my dad had said to me about not compromising your values. At the end of the day, when you check out of here in 70 or 80 years, and here I am now probably within 15 or 20 years, hopefully, of the end of life on this Earth, he said to me for years that the only thing that you get to keep is who you are.

Even though I spent the next year trying to figure it out, I think I spent that senior year in '68, '69, trying to figure out ways to not face who I was. But I already knew, that summer day after Kennedy was shot. I'm not going to go shoot somebody that I don't know, that I can't figure out any reason, they've never done anything to hurt me. I don't think that anybody crawling around in a rice field in Vietnam is gonna have any clear and present danger to the United States. And I'm not going.

I taught for a year and a half, I lost my deferment, and when you lose your deferment, you got a brief deferment—I think it was like 90 days or something—in which to file. I wrote my letter. I filed for conscientious objection.

My intention had always been to go into law, and I was a government, political science, and history major. I had a pretty good understanding of law and conventions and how things worked. To be honest, I knew from the very beginning that conscientious objection at that time in the United States was primarily for Quakers and Seventh-Day Adventists who objected to all war. And even when I wrote my statement, I said, I don't necessarily object to all war. If the United States was being attacked, if we were being invaded, there was a clear national interest and my family, my culture, my society was being threatened, would I defend it? Probably I would.

But in this situation, when I look at what's happening in Vietnam, where it's being fought for some theoretical thing of stopping the domino effect of countries falling to communism—which is even questionable, whether fighting wars against that works, which, as we've seen in Iraq and Afghanistan, it doesn't do particularly well—I said, I'm a selective conscientious objector. The truth of the matter is that under US law, there was no provision for someone to be a selective conscientious objector. The only way you could truly qualify for it was to object on all grounds to all war at all times. Jehovah's Witnesses, for example, they will not take a loyalty oath to a government to fight, under any circumstances. That's really what the conscientious objection provisions of the draft law were intended to cover: Jehovah's Witnesses, Quakers, Seventh-Day Adventists, people who object to all war. There was no provision for selective conscientious objection, not legally.

So it was kind of a Catch-22. People asked me, well, why apply for something that you know in advance that you won't get, that you'll lose this. And not only will you lose it, you already know that you should lose it, legally? Because I knew I didn't qualify for conscientious objection. I was a selective conscientious objector. It came back to the same thing. It was Buffy Sainte-Marie; it was my dad who said do a gut check and make sure that you're doing the right thing, that you're being true to yourself. And I said, here's the truth: if our country were attacked, I'd defend it. But that's not happening, and I'm not going to do it. I'm not going.

» The one other seminal thing that happened was I was married. I had a young wife. It was a relatively new relationship. We married in June of '69, and by the fall of 1970 I was facing this decision because, you know, we were a couple. Whatever decision I was making, she was going through it too. My wife was fully supportive of me. Never blinked.

There's that story about Pierre Trudeau. I don't know what decision he was making, but he supposedly walked out in the snow in Ottawa and took a long walk one night, and we did the same thing. In about December of 1970, we were living in a farmhouse, kind of being pretend hippies, out in the country outside of St. Louis, and we took a walk in the snow, and by the time we got back we went, Okay, this is what's going to happen. If I get drafted, I'm not going to step forward; I'm going to refuse. They're going to arrest me, they're going to interview me, they're going to release me, and then it'll take a couple of years, and there will be a case. We agreed that that was the thing to do.

Both of my parents were Midwestern Republicans. Both went, "You know, if you've got a felony conviction, are you going to be able to have a teaching certificate? Where is your career going to go? Are you going to be accepted back into this community? You're teaching in this conservative, small Midwestern community." You know, all the things that everybody who became a conscientious objector or a draft dodger ever heard were always, you know, they brought them all up. All the standard middle-class parents' things to bring up: care about the kids' future and "You're stepping way off the traditional path here, pal," and you're going to have professional and personal consequences that come with this.

They were worried about what was going to happen to me. But I happened to run across a thing that my dad wrote today, with pluses and minuses, a list. He was big on doing a T-chart when he had to make decisions. Okay, what're the best outcomes? And what are the worst outcomes? It's about eight points long. But it wasn't ever presented to me as "This is what you should do." When I was ten years old, other kids would get in trouble, and my parents, my dad particularly, would say,

"So, when you make this kind of a decision"—whatever it was that I had done, it was usually probably something that was not the wisest choice that I had ever made—"so what do you think can happen when you make a decision like that?" I was never grounded, didn't know physical punishment, ever. Then in mid-adolescence, when other kids were struggling with parents and having these big battles over curfews and stuff like that—I mean that was the big thing in the mid-60s, what time do you have to be in, right?—my dad would go, "Well you gotta be in by a reasonable time." I'd go, "Well what time is that?" And he'd go, "You know when that would be. Figure it out." He said, "If it gets to be a problem, I'll let you know."

That moved me forward, again with this thing of "You've gotta live with the consequences of your decisions." Am I going to man up? Am I going to accept the consequences for my decision? It wasn't just about being a CO [conscientious objector]; it was the whole ball of wax.

Then it entered into, like, crazy world. I'm coming out of this small Midwestern town. You could probably have gotten the count of conscientious objectors that the local draft board had ever dealt with on two hands, for sure—maybe on the one hand. Basically, you came out of high school, you either got drafted or you enlisted. And a lot of my guys, we were football players, we were big tough guys, and the thing was, well, if I'm going to go, I'm going Marines, because those are the toughest and I can do it. To have someone come along then, especially, it was challenging, I think, for some people in my community because I was a leader in the community. If it were somebody that nobody noticed it would have been one thing, but when the quarterback of the football team was going "I ain't going," that definitely raised some attention in the community, not all of it positive.

When I lost my deferment, I was already five years out of high school, four years of college and a year of teaching while I was on deferment. Most of my friends who didn't go to university either enlisted or were drafted right out of high school. Of course, the people who were most supportive of me being a conscientious objector were friends of mine who had been in Vietnam. I didn't ever try to hide what I was doing, even though I knew, in general, this was not a cool thing to do, not at all.

I had moms of friends of mine on the draft board that I eventually had to appeal to: people whose houses I'd visited to have cookies and milk in their kitchens since I was ten years old.

I talked to one white friend who had enlisted in the Marines, and four Black friends who had been drafted and were in army infantry. When I told them about it, they just went, "You know what, man, if I had had the opportunity and the support to do that, knowing what I know now... We didn't know anything. We were 17 years old. Knowing what I know now, I'd have been doing the same thing that you are right now." And they were the main support that I had through that three-year battle with the draft board.

You ask for letters of support. I asked my high school principal, who I was very close to as student body president, had a great relationship, but he was a conservative guy. I asked him for a letter of support for my conscientious objection. I said, "You know me, you know I act on principles, and you know I'm sincere." And he wrote a letter to the draft board going, "Don't give it to him. He doesn't realize how bad he's messing up his life." And he said, "I have no doubt that he's sincere, but he's making a horrible mistake." He wrote a three-page letter to the draft board on why they shouldn't give it to me.

I went to my pastor, the pastor of the church. He did support me. And interestingly, my dad, because he knew that even though he disagreed with it, he was going to support me.

» So the first thing that happens is they reclassify. Because you've had a teacher deferral, they have to make you 1-A so that they can draft you. And the first thing they sent, it was 1-A, you are drafted. I'm submitting my conscientious objection application. I submitted it. They turned me down and sent me a draft notice. So I got draft notice number one. I appealed it and said no, you made a mistake. Well, at that point you have to have a hearing. I went to the hearing, and that was the wildest affair ever, to sit down in a room with leaders in your small community. And at the initial hearing they offered me what is called 1-A-O.

That was sort of an out for draft boards. If you objected to going as a conscientious objector—which is 1-O—they could classify you as 1-A-O, which means you would still be drafted, but you were guaranteed that you would be in a support role, that you'd be a medic, that you wouldn't be armed. And of course, during that meeting, they said, "Well, we don't believe you, that you are a conscientious objector, but we will give you a 1-A-O." They've got a quota. Every draft board had a certain number of people that they had to draft each month. Like my town, they had to have 18 people from the draft board that they took. If you were 1-A-O, you were still drafted, you still counted towards their draft quota. But to be 1-A-O, I've still got to step forward and join the army, to take an oath of loyalty that I will follow orders and the US military.

At that point, my thinking was solidified a lot more, and I went, "I'm not going to swear allegiance to an organization that I don't believe in." My thinking was getting clearer as I was going through this process. I said, "I have no problem doing volunteer service for two years in a civilian hospital. I'll work at a veterans hospital with the most difficult patients. I'll do any work that you want, but I'm not going to become a member of the military." And I think I said something in that hearing, that I just don't trust this anymore. I don't know, yeah, you're a medic, and you're under fire, and someone throws a gun to you and says, "Help your friends." I would still put myself in the position halfway around the world in a fight that I don't have any understanding of the reason for. I'm not going to do it. At that point I said, "Not only will I not kill anybody in this war. I'm not swearing allegiance to the army because I don't believe that they are operating in our best interests. I don't trust this. I won't go, and I won't be part of your draft quota." And they turned me down, and they drafted me a second time. So I had draft notice number two.

My status was still 1-A, and they drafted me for the second time. At that point, the Supreme Court had ruled, in the United States, that if draft boards were going to turn somebody down for conscientious objection, they had to put a letter in the file giving their rationale for why they did it. You can't just turn it down and go, "Pfft, get out of here; you're going to 'Nam." They had to state the reason why they did not give it. Somehow, they forgot to file the letter for me.

They made a legal mistake. On top of that, my mom had done her master's work. She taught public speaking. And for her master's work, she had analyzed the speeches of Senator Stuart Symington of Missouri, who at that time happened to be the head of the Senate Foreign Relations

Committee for the United States. She also sent a letter to him, saying there was no letter put into my file stating why they had turned me down. That's a violation. So he sent a request to the local board that it be reopened for the third time. They considered it for the third time. They turned it down. I appealed it. The second appeal hearing was very brief. Oh, they did not want to see me. They did not want to see my face at that point.

I knew the senator had sent them a letter saying, "You guys messed up, you didn't say why you didn't give him his conscientious objector status." They could have easily done it. All they'd have to say in the letter was, well, he clearly states that he is not 100 percent a conscientious objector, he's a selective objector to the war in Vietnam. They could have done it quite easily. They filed the letter, put it in my file, and they drafted me for the third time.

When I started dealing with the case was late 1970, until spring of '72. It was stressful for me and my wife; it definitely put stresses and strains. You're going, you're not going, you're going to get arrested. We did think about the possibility of moving to Canada at that point. I had known lots of people that had. But again, it was a matter of being true to myself. I never really entertained it. I should finish that process.

I got drafted for the third time for something like, I believe, November 8 or 10, 1972, but the draft law expired on October 31, 1972. And Congress was at that point fed up with it. That was after Nixon had said that they weren't in Cambodia, except that they had 50,000 guys in Cambodia. All the lying that had gone on—everyone in Congress at that point was going, "We're not sending anybody else, we're done with this." Meanwhile, Nixon was still carrying on the war.

So the draft law expired on October 31, and Congress wouldn't renew it. So here I was sitting, there were no more options, there were no more appeals, I had my day in court, I lost, I should have lost—not my day in court, my day with the draft board—and the draft law expired. Which meant any draft notices that had been sent after October 31 weren't valid because they didn't have any legal authority to call up anybody after that. So by about ten days, I missed being drafted. At that point I would not have stepped forward and taken the oath. Then I would have been in court. It was something that we thought was going to end very dramatically with getting interviewed by the FBI. And it was a little letter that said, "Okay, pal, but if there is another war, if something else breaks out, don't think you're off the hook. Basically, you're going to be at the top of our list" kind of thing.

We did read about coming to Canada. One of my college roommates—his number was, like, 4 when they did the draft lottery, so he knew, like, the day he was out of college, the next month he was going to be drafted. He enlisted. He did really well. He went to advanced infantry training. He was the soldier of the month. He went to Airborne [the Airborne Division of the US Army] at Fort Bragg in North Carolina and won the soldier of the month again. And his reward for being the soldier of the month and being featured on the front page of the little base magazine was you got three days off. Your parents and your girlfriend could come and see you, and there was a big award ceremony, and you got three days off before you went to Vietnam. Well, in the three days off, he went to Toronto.

He was what they call AWOL: he was away without leave. He was a deserter. He was already in the army, and then he couldn't even go back for visits. So I knew people who had gone to Canada. We could have easily packed up and driven across the border and never looked back. The reason that I didn't do it at that time was because of the support and friendship of the veterans who had supported me in my conscientious objector case. I kind of went, okay, here are these guys who have seen it all, who were shot at, who did crawl through the mud, had been sprayed with Agent Orange. Those are the guys that are supporting me, so what am I going to do? Walk out of the country? I don't think so. I can't do that. They've been my greatest support.

So we didn't flee the country to avoid the draft. Technically, I'm not a draft dodger in the sense that I went to Canada. I'm a draft dodger in the sense that I took every legalistic method that I could take to avoid going. The other thing that I was acutely aware of during that period when I was going through that case, I was aware of my white privilege.

So the war resistance was the flame that lit the possibility of looking at Canada. My roommate had done it; I had known other people. I had gone to a draft counsellor who helped me prepare my case, and they're all sitting there going, "Okay, middle-class white guy, don't worry about this too much. If it all goes south at the end, we can have you in Toronto in 48 hours. No problem. You can always cross the border." So the whole idea of moving to Canada came out of war resistance.

At that point, I was making probably $6,500 a year. We were really struggling. That summer we decided to do a quick camping tour, and we went from Chicago. Neither of us had ever been to Canada. Let's just cross the border south of Winnipeg and go there and see it. We got there and went, wow, there's no traffic, it's quiet, the teacher salaries are better than the Midwest. The Americans that we're meeting up here are primarily people who think a lot like us because they're here because they fled the war, or made the decision to go back to the land, one or the other. Can you come up with three good reasons why we would not move to Canada? And we really couldn't come up with any. So the spark of looking at Canada because of war resistance was then fuelled by people we met when we came up here.

We came to Canada in '75, and we came to Nelson in '81.

» I had to call my son two weeks ago and have a conversation about "the Talk": this is when Black families have a young Black male, having "the Talk" when you go, "Listen, you get stopped by police, you keep your hands on the steering wheel, you answer the question, don't talk back. If there is a problem and something is being done improperly, your lawyer can handle it the next day. But don't try haggling at the roadside because bad things happen."

And you know, that talk should never have to take place. I mean, even the fact that here I am, as a Caucasian teacher of 48 years, a principal, sitting in a half-million-dollar house, and I gotta call my kid, and he's 40, and go, "Be careful if you get stopped." But you do need to. And I found that that part of American culture, more than anything, pushed me back. I've had some interesting experiences going back on occasion. The power structure in the States: after all these years, they're still harassing guys just because they're Black. When I look back, I have no question that my move to Canada was part of being true to myself. I started with the war resistance, but it's become a lot more than that. It about what the culture's about.

I've spoken to a lot of friends about the Truth and Reconciliation Commission of Canada. Honestly, when I came to Canada I didn't know what a residential school was. But, you know, you can't go back and fix any of that stuff; horrible things were done, horrible things were done. But at least Canada has acknowledged it, said we destroyed families, we actively attempted to destroy a culture. We committed at least cultural, and in some cases physical, genocide. We acknowledge it. We apologize for it. And we want to make amends as best as possible this far in the future and move forward.

In the US, particularly across the race divide, no one is teaching it in high school—"By the way, we lynched 5,000 Black men." Nobody wants to say it. I've found myself feeling this is important as I get older: no one talks about some of the real tragedies and divisions racially, and between the rich and the poor.

I'm so happy that I've raised my children in a place where, it's not perfect by a long shot, but I feel like, as a culture, there is an attempt to acknowledge mistakes. To not be so critical about people because they're different, they go about things in a different way. Another thing, with accepting Syrian refugees, Canada has done a lot more. It's a big, big difference.

But it was hard. There is a classic picture of my mom with the two kids in her arms, saying goodbye as we left St. Louis to move to Alberta. Now, when I look at the look on her face, it was full of anguish. The decision that I made created real anguish for her and her grandchildren. Instead of being down the block, we're gonna be 2,000 miles away. There are prices for every decision. And for my wife, over the years I underestimated how much she missed the closeness of her biological family.

I think that for a lot of draft dodgers, war resisters, or people who just moved sparked by the war in Vietnam, Afghanistan, or Iraq, there is a family price that you pay. You build a new family; you live in a new culture. And over time that gets gentler and gentler. But there are losses in that kind of immigration. Both my wife and I were very fortunate that my war resistance didn't create a gulf with our families. The distance did to some extent, just because we weren't in physical contact all that often. But both families fully accepted that. We did what we did; we were who we were. I don't have any regrets, but I think that anybody you would talk to is mixed with joy and sadness.

Lee at a protest against the deportation of American war resisters. (Photo by Ian Willms. Used with permission.)

8 Lee

I WAS BORN IN BROOKLYN, NEW YORK, in 1944, and spent most of my youth on Long Island.

My father fought in WW II and remained in the Air Force Reserve afterwards, so that he was often on training missions. When I was young, his attitude towards the military, however, was skeptical. He enjoyed it, but he didn't respect the hierarchy.

I was somewhat active in local politics. I went to many of the demonstrations, and I was opposed to the war. Of course I realized that I could be drafted, because every male was liable for that. I had to register with the draft board and go for a physical. I was going to university at that time, and I got deferments, but they eventually ran out in 1969. I had to report changes in status to the draft board, so I sent in my report and literally within three days the draft notice came to my house. They were desperate at that time in my draft board area. Most of the young men went to college, so they had a very small pool of people to draw from. The minute somebody became available, they immediately picked him up. On February 6, 1969, I reported to some location in Manhattan and was inducted into the United States Army, along with several hundred other guys.

I opposed the war pretty much from 1965 on. So when I got notice, I had to consider whether I would obey or not. I knew that some people went to Canada, and I thought maybe I could do the same. But I decided to answer the call and comply. I was surrounded in the northeastern United States with people who were opposed to the war, and we all agreed on that. But I wondered, if I was exposed to a broader selection of Americans, whether I would question my point of view. Also, I was American. My country had given me a number of benefits, and maybe I should repay. So I did not go to Canada.

I started my service very soon after in Fort Jackson, South Carolina. I stayed at the base as a soldier until the end of 1969.

Once I got into the army, very soon I realized that in fact my opposition to the Vietnam War was right: the war was wrong. What I heard from guys who had been over there and returned was not remotely reassuring.

I eventually put in a conscientious objector application, based on the idea that I didn't oppose war in general necessarily, but I opposed this war because it was immoral and illegal. That was processed through the army bureaucracy. The denial rate for those is about 98 percent, and I was one of the 98 percent. You have to go through various steps. When I had an interview with a chaplain, for example, I could see that he was trying to trap me into admitting that I was afraid. He asked me, "Would you be afraid of going to Vietnam and maybe getting killed or wounded?" And I said, "Yes, of course." And he made a note that he had "got" me.

So the answer came back "no." I appealed. Finally, the answer came back "no." I was sent to advanced infantry training, completed that, and that's when my orders came down.

I received orders to go to Fort Lewis, Washington, to be shipped to Vietnam in early December of '69. It was at that time that I began to focus pretty intensely on what I would do in response.

During training, I was exposed to a broader sample of Americans, Southerners particularly: African Americans. This was America, and I found that very enlightening in many ways, but none of it gave me the idea that the war was right. The attitude of most of them was: Well, you got to do it and survive. You have two years, then you get out and go on with your life.

There was a lot of minor resistance to the army generally. The slogan FTA was widely spread, written on walls, and constantly repeated verbally. FTA stands for "Fuck the Army." So the sergeants would say, "You got an FTA attitude, do some push-ups or something." Men would constantly give the peace sign and other things. These were not young men who were necessarily opposed to the war or had a position on it. They simply were swept up in the youth movement, which was opposed to the war. And they didn't want to go. Some from the South saw it as maturing: you go home in uniform, and it makes a man of you. Mostly it was: "Don't get upset about it, just do the job, do what they tell you. Don't make waves. Get out of here."

Knowledge about Canada was widespread in the army. There was that well-known *Manual for Draft-Age Immigrants to Canada* which circulated, and I had seen a copy and read it. So I was aware of the option when I was given my orders.

Normally, they handed you your orders and 50 copies, and you were supposed to bring it with you to the next place you were assigned. They didn't do that with me because they didn't trust me to keep the orders, because maybe I would throw them away. Because I had been—in a small way—resisting the war within the military, and they knew about it. I had been interrogated by an intelligence sergeant on camera. He said, "You know, there were some Cubans in town a few weeks ago. Did you get in contact with them?" And I said, "No!" But he did show me photographs they had taken from across the street from the anti-war G.I. Cafe on Assembly Street in Columbia, South Carolina, where I had been photographed entering and leaving.

I was known to them as a dissident, so they didn't hand me my orders; they sent them on ahead of me. I was given the date to appear at Fort Lewis, Washington, on January 1 at midnight 1970: "Happy New Year." Then you usually get a leave to go home and take care of any business or whatever before you go overseas.

So I got out, and I began thinking about what I should do. I didn't want to go. I had decided I really didn't want to go. Do I do it by refusing to go and getting processed through the legal system, maybe jail or something? Or do I go to Canada? I called a pro-G.I., very good lawyer and asked them what they thought of the idea of me going to the base, reporting for duty, and bringing one of the lawyers with me so he could witness my refusal of the orders. He said, "We can't promise that. We have no right to be on the base. They can simply tell us to go away. And you would be alone. And if you're alone, the army has legal right to physically compel you."

I knew of a case like that, so I decided, "That's not an option, so I guess it's Canada."

My father became impatient and said, basically, "Shit or get off the pot. Make your decision." He was an impatient guy, so this was pretty common behaviour on his part, but he wasn't saying I shouldn't go.

I thought about it for a few weeks, and eventually I made arrangements.

My father was distressed that I made the decision to go to Canada. My mother was supportive and didn't try to convince me not to go. But many years later I realized that it had been a severe blow to her, that she had always expected me to be near her when I grew up, and I wasn't. Very much later, when my father died, I rushed down to Florida where they were living at that time to be with her. With my sister present, my mother had occasion to call me a selfish bastard. I think what she meant was that I took my own ideals and set it above my family obligations to her, my mother. For that reason, I was selfish. She never berated me for doing it because I deserted my country; it was more a matter of the family dynamics that ensued. My grandmother, her mother, on the other hand, visited me unannounced while I was in the army. And she was quite a woman. She came up from Puerto Rico to South Carolina, unannounced. She showed up at the base demanding to know where her grandson was. Eventually, we were united. Her attitude when I deserted was seen as, Well, better a live coward than a dead hero. That was how my family reacted generally. They didn't try to stop me or argue with me, but it was a blow to them.

» I got on a bus and went to Buffalo. I stayed the first night there. This was partly to distract and throw the FBI off my trail—I mean, I'm just going to Buffalo. I bought a bus ticket from Buffalo to Toronto and took the bus the next day. There was no problem.

I came in as a visitor, and when I got to Toronto I rented a room and began thinking about how I would get processed to be a landed immigrant. What I needed was information from back home—for example, my university grades. Unfortunately, at that very moment, the first and only nationwide postal strike began in the United States and lasted for quite a while. So I had to wait for that to be over so that my university could mail my transcripts.

I had been in touch with the Toronto Anti-Draft Programme, and they arranged for me to go to a location in Welland, Ontario, not too far from the border, where they had a "safe house." I slept one night on the floor there with a large number of other people. The next morning I was taken to a convent or a seminary right on the border overlooking the Niagara River, where I was met by an American woman. I'm sorry I don't remember her name because she played a big role in my life.

She had a New York licence plate. The idea was we would pretend that we were returning to the United States from a quick visit to Niagara Falls, and that she was my mother's friend, that's why I knew her.

I was very frightened, scared to death of going back into the United States. And dealing with the officials there. If they had discovered that I was a deserter, they might well have arrested me, and I would have been sent back to the army and punished or just sent to Vietnam. Luckily, that didn't happen.

The plan would have fallen apart in two seconds if the border guard had begun inquiring. But he did not. He just waved us through. She made a U-turn back to the Canadian border station, and I got out of the car with my documentation. I went in and said I'd like to apply for landed immigrant status. They interviewed me, assessed me according to the point system, and I was granted landed immigrant status then and there. I then got back into her car. She took me to the dropping-off point, I got back on the bus and went to Toronto as a landed immigrant in Canada. That's how easy it was.

» My attitude was: I am now a new Canadian, I'm not an American exile. I'm not sitting here thinking, waiting for the day it becomes possible to return home. This is my home now. So rather than get involved in the exile community as many did, I got involved in activism in Canada. I never have experienced a wish to go back to the United States, except on visits to see my parents or for the War Resisters Support Campaign. Other than that, I've never had the temptation.

I was 24 years old when I entered Canada. When I was a kid, we took a trip to Quebec City, so I had some memory of that: it was quaint. I didn't know anything about Toronto except what I had read in that manual.

I got involved in the NDP in the provincial campaigns. I was pretty well integrated into the NDP and into the local community downtown. I decided I would try to get a master's degree, so I went to University of Toronto and got a master's in Russian history.

I needed money, so eventually I became a cab driver. Many new immigrants who are English-speaking become cab drivers. I got involved in a small group of people, drivers, who were trying to get a union going. I became active in that. I used to go to the taxi stands and try to sign up guys to be members. We did quite a bit of organizing. We set ourselves up in the CUPE headquarters. We set up a table and we signed up hundreds of guys.

That's how my activism got started in Canada. I carried on that way for the most part, with some breaks. You know, sometimes I just have to withdraw. You get burned out and so on. But with some breaks, I've continued with the activism ever since.

» The first memory I have of resisters coming to Canada from the Iraq War is that I got an email from Michelle. There were some Iraq War resisters coming to Canada, and a group was starting to give them support and help them to stay in Canada, and she invited me to a meeting. I went to the meeting, and I knew some of the people from activism before. It sounded like a very good cause to me. I met the first Iraq War resister, Jeremy Hinzman, and he's a very impressive person. I decided to get involved.

Then it turned out that we were able to get some space at the Steelworkers Hall to open a little office. They needed somebody to staff it part-time, so I volunteered to do that, and I used my savings to support myself, along with a hundred-dollar weekly stipend from the Campaign. My role was to come to the office every day in the afternoon and deal with the phone calls, media and maybe war resisters, potential war resisters calling for information. Also, I would take on various things, such as if they needed a speaker over here, we're doing this over there, we're going to set up a table to get signatures on our petition. I would go help out with that and so on.

Eventually, more war resisters started coming. Many of them would call the office first, and I would answer their questions as best I could and tell them we could not guarantee anything, they may have to go back eventually. That this was their decision. And we reinforced that so that they knew the risks they were taking when they came to Canada.

When they did come, we went out of our way to house them, provide some funds, some kind of a social context, meet the other guys and hang out to give them a support network and involve them in the activism if they were interested. In many cases we involved them in dealing with the media. The media desperately wanted to speak with them: they were American soldiers who opposed the war and had done something about it. This is a combination that didn't exist almost anywhere else. So the world media became very interested, and we had reporters come from all over—from Japan, Tasmania. A guy came from Tasmania to Toronto to learn about it. There was interest from TV networks all over the States: CNN, CBS, you name it. We had war resisters speaking on those, and my job was to sort of stickhandle that in such a way as they would, you know, be giving their full consent. We told them, "Look, this is up to you. You don't want to do it? Fine, no problem with us. You didn't come to Canada to be a media star." But surprisingly enough, most of them did want to do that.

I do think some found it a burden. These were not people who were show-offs and trying to be big celebrities or anything like that. But to give them credit, they did it. They travelled the country, speaking at all kinds of events to all kinds of audiences. We went across the country, from Newfoundland to Nova Scotia to BC, with the war resisters. We had friends and supporters in various parts of Canada that took them under their wing. When the resisters would visit, they would house them, bring them to the media to give them that support.

One of the war resisters wrote a book. Josh Key was being interviewed on CBC when the writer Lawrence Hill was listening, and he heard Josh's story. So he got in touch with Josh, and they worked together on the book *The Deserter's Tale*. It became pretty well known at the time. It got reviewed in the *New York Review of Books*. These kind of stories went on for a number of years, until Obama got into office and the war started winding down and disappeared from the front pages in the United States pretty much. War resisters came less frequently to Canada because Obama was winding it down.

» We were then faced with the difficulty of dealing with the new government of Canada, which had been elected in 2006 and was Conservative. One of the basic beliefs among Conservatives is that being a soldier is a sacred thing, that you must be a gallant warrior or hero and never give up and never turn tail. All that mythology is part of conservatism.

The Stephen Harper Government was determined to deport every war resister that they could. They regarded [hosting war resisters] as an insult to the United States, which, of course, Canada should not do. They regarded the refugee claims that were being made as, in a word used by the immigration minister, "bogus." He said that publicly. We had a long battle ahead of us.

We had been making some progress with the Liberal government that was in office up to that time. We were in touch with the immigration minister, and he told us that he was working on it and was about to make some kind of a comment in Cabinet about it and try to move the ball forward. So we were sort of optimistic that with a lot of work and a lot of organizing and lobbying we could push the government to make this possible to let them stay.

When Harper came in, that all changed. There was just no possibility they would speak with us. They regarded us as the enemy, as an embarrassment to Canada, and Harper was in for nine, ten years. While we were still lobbying and building support among Canadians and the world, we were forced to be on the defensive. There were repeated incidents where war resisters would reach a certain stage in their immigration and refugee processing and then were denied, and maybe they would be deported. We had to decide if we could appeal it in the Federal Court, if in fact the Federal Court agreed to hear it. If they agreed to hear it, then perhaps we could get a victory or, as they did in a number of cases, order a new refugee hearing and begin the process from the start again, gaining time.

And so that's what we did. And we were very lucky to run into somebody who committed herself to this effort: Alyssa Manning. Alyssa used her brilliant mind and her extreme level of hard work to build cases for each of the war resisters that came, that were threatened in this way. She did a fantastic job. On one occasion she was all ready with her materials and everything, and went to Federal Court that day. We all turned out to show support. The federal lawyer came in and said, "We're not doing the trial today." I think they were just afraid to lose again. One time I asked Alyssa, "This is probably taking up a lot of your time," and she said, "I'm committed." She's a woman of relatively few words for a lawyer. And what she said was true: she was committed. We were lucky. So we won some cases, and we prolonged some cases until the Harper Government fell and was replaced.

In other cases, we failed: the circumstances didn't work out so that the person could go to Federal Court. One of those was Robin Long, who was arrested in Nelson, BC. He had been on a Canada-wide warrant for his arrest because he hadn't turned up at an appointment at immigration. We put up as much agitation and demonstration as possible out in Vancouver. Our supporters out there got together and raised some hell. But it was too late. Robin was deported, and he served a little over a year in jail. I think Robin would certainly have wanted to remain in Canada and have access to his son.

There were other examples like that. I would say the most prominent one was Kim Rivera, who went through a lot of processing and hearings but eventually ran out of options. She had to decide whether she would go into sanctuary like Rodney Watson did in Vancouver. There were churches that were willing to help. It's a big, big thing for a church to do that. But there were some that we could have worked with. However, Kim decided that she would comply with a deportation order if she got one. Eventually, the order came, and she did leave with her family and was taken into custody at the border. She was jailed away from her small children for almost a year. When that happened, it was announced by the immigration minister in the House [Parliament] that Kim Rivera had finally left Canada. All the members on the Tory benches stood up and cheered. Kim had a baby in jail, in the stockade. I think that was one of the most disheartening and disgraceful things that the Harper Conservatives did: to revel in the pain and suffering of this young woman, this young mother, is, I think, beyond contempt.

Meanwhile, we had been lobbying Parliament, and it was a minority Parliament, two minority Parliaments in a row. In both of them, we got motions passed by a majority asking the government to make provision for the war resisters to stay in Canada. The government, of course, ignored it. It was not binding, and they ignored it. However, we have always felt that the Canadian people were essentially behind us, although they weren't necessarily very vocal about it. I mean, they certainly were not objecting to war resisters staying in Canada, except for the Tory base, as they call it. They were outraged that anyone could take an oath of military service and then disregard it. When I spoke with some of them I would ask, "Do you believe in divorce? You think we should reverse the divorce laws and stop divorce because, you know, when you say 'till death do us part' is a little stronger than 'I promise to serve in the United States Army for three years.'" I would say the biggest issue that they used against us was that persons in the US volunteered. Without knowing the context, it sounds really conclusive. But, in fact, most people volunteered because they had no other options.

So there was our activism. This was partly because of Michelle, and partly because it was simply what was necessary to be done. It involved everything from rallying support in all the possibly sympathetic organizations: the trade unions, the churches, human rights organizations, Amnesty International, lobbying Members of Parliament, and so on.

Eventually, Stephen Harper lost the election in 2015, and Justin Trudeau came in. We had been lobbying the Liberals for a long time. I think Corey even met with Trudeau before he was leader, along with some other members of the Liberal caucus. I remember we made a trip up to Ottawa and met with them to try to push them to endorse our campaign. We were talking about getting a bill through Parliament and lining up parties behind it. But that was only one side of our activity.

At the same time, we were dealing with war resisters who might have a housing problem and might have some other health problem or God knows what. We were providing services as best we could to them, and maintaining a network of people across the country. We were doing as much media as we could possibly do and all that sort of stuff. This was a small group, but very active. It was, I would say, probably the best campaigning that I've ever seen done, given our resources and given the obstacles that we had with a government that was openly hostile to us.

Once the Liberals got in, they moved slowly, but they did move, and eventually war resisters were given permanent resident status. So they're going to be Canadians now, and this is their choice. These are good people; Canada's lucky to get them. They're going to be good Canadians and add to this country.

» I always told the people right up front that I had been through some of it too. I told them that it was a lot easier in my day to become a permanent resident. That's why we had to put up this big fight. Because of my army experience, I would talk a little army with them. But aside from that, I think it was a bond that I had with them. When they would first come here, they'd be afraid, they wouldn't know who we were. I told them, "I came up during Vietnam, and I want you to know that I love you. I'm not in love with you, but I do love you because you're a war resister like me." I don't know if they all cottoned to that very well, but I wanted them to understand that we were dealing with them as individuals on the basis of intimacy and feeling, not just a bureaucratic organization that sees them as a number and so forth.

I am gay and I told them that too, so they wouldn't find out behind my back and think that I was trying to hide it. But I told them that I'm not in love with you, not to worry about it. It was probably a bit foolish of me to say those things, but I think it was best to be honest and open and try to give them a feeling that the people here weren't just a bunch of ideological pricks, using them as a way to screw the government or something like that. This is the way the United States tried to portray us.

» Why did [the Campaign] attract a number of gay people? I think it's because some gays are sort of radical. In my case, I'm gay and I was a Vietnam War resister, so that's my reason. It was an overrepresentation of gays as compared with the population in general. And I think that's something to be proud of. I didn't know if any of the war resisters were gay. Maybe some were. That was part of the deal: if they were coming to Canada and they were working with us, they had to maybe make adjustments of their perspective to allow for the fact that they were working with some gay people who are openly gay.

In my day, you didn't just check a box [to say that you were gay and get out of service]. You had to prove it. And usually you'd have to get a letter from somebody [saying] that you had sex. How do you prove you're gay?

The army was wise to the idea that if all of a sudden all of America's young men turned out to be gay, we can't have a war. There were some guys who might have said they were gay who weren't. They might have been able to arrange some form through a doctor or psychiatrist or something. I don't know. I don't think I knew anybody like that.

I knew one gay man in my company who was very flamboyant. I think he was that way all the time. He wasn't just putting it on. They [the military] felt they had to get rid of him, get him out of the army quickly. So they took him out of our barracks and put him in the commanding general's office to sleep until they could process him out. If he was in our barracks, presumably there would have been a massive sex orgy with him or something. So that was one extreme.

The other extreme would have been people like me who were gay but were not out. My conscientious objection was real, and I didn't want to sort of skirt around it by saying that I'm gay and making that the issue. I wanted the issue to be my opposition to the war. It may have been just an excuse not to come out and be embarrassed coming out. But on the other hand, I think it was valid.

» As far as my career in Canada, I was an activist, and my first campaign was working in Jack Layton's office when he was in his first term as a city councillor back in the early '80s, and I was his executive assistant, and then for my MP. After that I worked at a community health centre at Queen and Bathurst as a community health organizer and advocate. I was a very disruptive element.

Then I worked at the AIDS Committee of Toronto for a few years. I wasn't very happy there. Eventually, I quit there and I had plenty of free time. So I worked for the war resisters. That's the kind of career I had.

» In 2008, I was friends with a young Vietnamese guy who had just got married. He was going back to Vietnam to introduce his wife to his family. He hadn't seen them for five years. He asked me if I wanted to go to Vietnam, and I did. I met some people that he knew. I decided the next year to go back, and I've gone back every winter since. I think it's ten times now, and I spend usually two months there every time. I've come to know it pretty well.

I went at first partly to see the world. And secondly, I think that my country, America, did some really bad things to Vietnam. I wanted to add something to Vietnam—maybe just being a tourist and spending money there. That helps, right? I didn't go as some people do to deal with feelings that they've been having or memories or even PTSD about their experiences in Vietnam, because I never fought there. But I still feel Vietnam had a major effect on my life.

If there had been no Vietnam War, I would no doubt have stayed in the United States. So it had a major effect on my life. When I went to Vietnam, I found the people are very nice and happy to see foreigners, partly because foreigners, they think, are rich. They may be able to make some money. But what I find in Vietnam is a kind of relaxation. It is a beautiful country. There's not much talk about the Vietnam War. A few older guys will say that they had been on the American side in the war and that it had spoiled their careers because the government never allowed them to get much opportunity. As far as my feeling about the war and my relation to it, I feel that it's a good thing that I give back something to the Vietnamese people, you know, by teaching English, by spending some money there.

In Vietnam, though, I know that there are organizations there that continue to do the work of reconciliation. For example, the Veterans for Peace have a place where kids who were affected by Agent Orange go.

I don't follow through on memories of Vietnam, but some guys do. To them, I think their resistance to the Vietnam War was a major turning point in their lives and they continue to work through that. Whereas I took the decision to come to Canada. I said, "I'm a new Canadian, I'm not an American exile."

I identify as Canadian. I have American citizenship because I didn't want to go through the red tape of renouncing it. I looked into it, but it costs money, and you have to fill out a lot of paperwork. What for? So, I have American citizenship. I don't vote in American elections. I don't pay American taxes. I haven't been to the United States in a number of years now. If the war resisters can't go, then I won't go unless it's on their business, something that the resisters' campaign is doing. But generally, I won't go anymore. I don't like it there. And I don't have a lot of money, so I can't travel everywhere. I save up all my money during the year to go to Vietnam. That's what I do.

Michelle, at right, holding the edge of a banner, with members of the War Resisters Support Campaign. (Photo courtesy of the War Resisters Support Campaign.)

9 Michelle

I GREW UP FOR THE FIRST FEW YEARS IN HULL, QUEBEC, and in Ottawa. My family is francophone. My father is from Quebec, and my mom is Franco-Ontarian.

The first time I ever was aware of Vietnam War resisters, I was quite young. I was seven. We lived in Toronto for a few years. In the house next door, four or five people lived there, and I thought of it as the hippie commune. But a number of the people there were Vietnam draft resisters who had come from Detroit. I always found it very interesting because they were grown-ups, but they were young grown-ups—they played cool music, and they had dogs. And so I was aware that there was something: they had to leave the United States to come to Canada. But, of course, I didn't understand what it all meant. Later, when I was back in Ottawa as a teenager, some of my best friends had a coach house, and a Vietnam deserter lived there. So it was very much part of the environment that I grew up in.

I'm one little piece of this giant period of effervescence and upheaval, where so many thousands of war resisters came up to Canada. But even in my little part of the world, or in my little existence, it touched me in a general way. And became part of how I saw the world: that Vietnam War resisters came to Canada.

When I was in high school, when I was 16, there was a woman named Anita Bryant who was an anti-gay crusader. And she was coming to Canada from the US to promote basically her homophobic message. I had started the first gay youth organization in Ottawa in my high school, with fellow students. So I was right into that, and I got involved in a coalition to protest against Anita Bryant coming to Ottawa. So that was 1978. There was a whole campaign that she was launching across North America, and that was our little piece of it in Ottawa. And that was my entry into sort of more formal activism. I'd been part of the grape boycott when I was in grade 7, I'd done things like that—but this was overtly political and more edgy than anything I had done before. And since then, it's been pretty much non-stop. I became a socialist. I was involved in the pro-choice movement, anti-war activism. So my whole life, basically since high school, I've been an activist. I've been a socialist, a radical.

There was a city-wide gay youth organization at the time. We didn't call it LGBTQ. This was 1978, and we were the first youth activists to start talking about that. It was before the time of gay-straight alliances and this type of discussion. In my high school, we had a number of openly gay students, and we had a rough time. But we had resources outside the school, which really helped us to get confident to do what we're doing. But that was just sort of my window into a much bigger political picture, which included a lot of different types of activism. And obviously most recently, I'd say the past 17 years of anti-war activism.

After 9/11, it was such a shock, such an earthquake, politically. I had been involved in the movement around globalization, and I'd been in Seattle for the WTO [World Trade Organization] protests in 1999. I'd been involved in this sort of global justice movement. And all of a sudden, everything felt like it screeched to a halt. The movement momentum just ground to a halt, and immediately what we understood is that we had to mobilize against this threat of war. In particular, I remember the slogan that came up was "Islam is not the enemy, and war is not the answer." And the whole thrust towards a war in Afghanistan. Why was a war in Afghanistan the solution that was being posed to what was obviously a criminal act? It was not a war. Why was a whole population going to be subjected to this, a population who had done nothing to deserve the kind of attack that they would soon be facing. So there were anti-war organizations that developed.

It took quite a while because there was a sense that somehow there was some legitimacy to this attack against Afghanistan. So I got involved in the anti-war organizing. And by the time the drumbeat of war against Iraq began, and the whole theme of weapons of mass destruction emerged, we had sizable organizations developed, and had had fairly large demonstrations.

That built up to February 15, 2003, which was probably the largest mobilization in human history. Millions of people in cities around the world protested against the looming war in Iraq. If Afghanistan was hard to understand as a target for a war, Iraq was even more so. What was the connection with 9/11? So that, for me, became the major part of my activity: organizing against the war. And ultimately, through the mobilizations that we did in Canada, we were able to prevent the Canadian government from participating in the so-called coalition of the willing.

In the process of organizing, here in Toronto and in other cities across the country, we did have a lot of interaction with US organizations who were similarly trying to mobilize. We had coordinated days of action between Canada and the US and actually around the world, like February 15, 2003. We developed connections with various anti-war groups. And after the initial invasion of Iraq in March of 2003, we continued, even though Canada wasn't participating directly in the invasion and occupation of Iraq. We continued to mobilize to participate in US actions. For example, we went to Washington in the fall of 2003. When we were there, we met activists who had started a group called Military Families Speak Out, which was basically an organization of families and loved ones of military personnel who were opposed to the war in Iraq. They used their position and their voice to particular effect to say that they didn't support the war. It really undermined the argument that opponents of the war didn't support the troops and started a real debate in the United States. Ultimately, those connections were important in the ongoing work afterwards when the first US war resisters arrived in Canada.

In January of 2004, we had invited the founders of Military Families Speak Out, Nancy Lessin and Charley Richardson, to come to Toronto to speak about their organization and their efforts to oppose the war, to really try to motivate people in Canada to continue to organize. We felt that their voices were particularly important, as families of US military personnel, in conveying what the cost of this war was and how it was being done in the teeth of opposition from military families. While they were here, a small article appeared in the *Globe and Mail* saying that the first resister to the Iraq War, the first US resister, had arrived in Toronto and claimed asylum. At that time, they introduced us to this individual, Jeremy Hinzman. And it occurred to us that this might become a thing, because the numbers that were being sent to Iraq were increasing. The occupation had been going on for a number of months, and the situation on the ground in Iraq was worsening. And so that was the beginning for us of thinking about what we could contribute to ensuring that people like Jeremy Hinzman could find refuge in Canada.

In March of 2004, we heard that a second US war resister had arrived: Brandon Hughey. And by the time he arrived, we had already found out something about the legal situation facing US war resisters. Unlike the previous generation who came during the Vietnam War, they couldn't simply apply at the border based on a point system and come into the country and get a work permit and so on. So when we met Brandon, it was really the moment when we decided we needed a separate campaign. Because at this point it really was anti-war activists across the country: people in Halifax, in Vancouver, connected through the Canadian Peace Alliance, who were thinking about this situation.

By May, we had assembled a small group of about 20 people—mostly Vietnam War resisters, some trade union activists, faith activists, and socialists, an imam from one of the mosques in Toronto—people from every different community.

On May 27, 2004, we held a press conference and launched the War Resisters Support Campaign. And obviously the networks that seemed natural to us to tap into were the people who had come up during the last wave of war resisters during the Vietnam War, and also the people who helped them at that time, who were a great resource for strategies for what we needed to do in identifying what was different between then and now.

There were two big currents that provided the foundation for our messaging and reaching out to people. The first was the very deep attachment that Canadians have to the history of welcoming Vietnam War resisters. You know, I'm just one person and I was touched by that. Even though I'm a bit younger than that generation, there are millions of Canadians who were touched by Vietnam War resisters coming to Canada, whether they were draft resisters or deserters. And so that was an obvious very, very, very deep attachment, but also very broad.

The other was the mass opposition to the Iraq War, which constituted a conduit of sympathy, because the Canadian population opposed the Iraq War. It was considered a statistical unanimity of Canadians opposing it, which just means that the vast majority of people opposed it. And these young men and women from the US military had also opposed this war. The speed with which the issue reached a quite wide public was remarkable to me. And in my experience of activism and organizing, this is something that was quite a rarity: the immense sympathy that people had for Iraq War resisters.

One of the most remarkable realizations for me, sitting where I am now, 14 years into this campaign to win asylum for Iraq War resisters, is the contrast between up to 100,000 Americans having come up during the Vietnam War and having been allowed to stay in one way or another—not without struggle and not without campaigning, but certainly the end result was that people were able to stay—this, and the small numbers of war resisters from the Iraq War, who have had to fight a ridiculously difficult battle with obstacles every step of the way over 14 years, and it's still not resolved. And what that has sort of taught us about what Canada really is, about the mythology of Canada as a safe haven; the degree to which we are having to fight tooth and nail to keep that legacy alive. Really what it tells you is that you cannot take for granted that something that may have existed in the past will continue.

In 2004, we began the Campaign under a Liberal government. When we said, "Pierre Trudeau in 1969 said that Canada should be a refuge from militarism. Surely the current Liberal government will see things the same way," we did not know the degree to which that was not the case. Canada was being blooded in the Afghanistan war; the Canadian government wanted troops to be tested on the ground and wanted to obliterate that history, frankly. And it wasn't just the subsequent Conservative government that did it, but it started under the Liberal government of Paul Martin and Jean Chrétien.

We can live in a fairy-tale world where Canada is a refuge from militarism. But it's not. And it wasn't really during the Vietnam War either. It was a struggle. It was interesting, digging into some of that history of what people had to do during the Vietnam War to be allowed to stay. There was a bit of a crapshoot: if you went to the border, you might not get in. You might be turned back. People who came here were being visited by the RCMP and being basically intimidated. Students at Glendon College had to go and do a whole operation, undercover, to show what was happening at the border with Canada when deserters arrived—that they were being turned back.

So all of these things were part of actually making Canada a "refuge from militarism" during the Vietnam War. And we had to go through a similar process, I think. The lessons of this are that, number one, you can't assume that because something was a particular way at one point that it continues. You have to struggle to maintain those gains. These gains are fragile. And there are forces out there that want to wipe them out. And number two, we can learn a lot from the history of how gains were made in the past, about how we can organize ourselves today to sustain those things, to build the kind of world that we want to see. And so, there are negative lessons, there are positive lessons. Ultimately, it's all been about struggle. We've had to struggle to keep the door, even this little opening, open today.

Something I discovered, which I did not know, was that draft resisters and deserters were treated differently in the early days of the Vietnam War when they came to Canada. Deserters were being sent back. They were being harassed and intimidated by the Canadian government in different ways.

I think that the rationale for the distinction between draft resisters and deserters was that desertion was something that was punishable, criminally, in Canada, as in the US. And that, therefore, was sort of upping the ante for the Canadian government to allow deserters, active-duty military personnel, to come into Canada during the Vietnam War. But the pressure was great. The moral rationale for not making that distinction was so obvious and glaring. If people are rejecting the draft because the war is wrong, because it's immoral, because it's illegal, then presumably someone who is walking away from the military for that reason, whether they were drafted or voluntarily enlisted, should also be allowed to stay.

I had been an activist for many years but had done very little lobbying. It was not something that particularly was my cup of tea. I was more interested in protests and that type of thing. But John Hagan's book *Northern Passage* talked about the lobbying that went on. A committee had been formed of prominent Canadians, people like Pierre Berton, June Callwood, and Farley Mowat. These are fairly well-known Canadian figures who were lobbying the government to allow war resisters to stay during the Vietnam War.

The second book that was quite important was called *Manual for Draft Age Immigrants to Canada*. It had been published in the 1960s by [House of Anansi Press and printed by] Coach House Press and it really was a "how to" guide for Vietnam War resisters: what they needed to do to come to Canada. From the point of view of the War Resisters Support Campaign, that was just beginning, many of us had never done this type of work where we had to think about the legal aspect for people coming to Canada. What was their status? How would they get status, housing, work, social support? All types of things that might not have been part of our activist lives before. So we spent some time looking at those things and thinking about what it told us about what had changed.

If you're an Iraq War resister coming to Canada in 2004, you couldn't apply at the border, in the way the Vietnam War resisters had been able to, to get permanent resident status in Canada (what used to be called landed immigrant status). You had to apply from outside the country. But if you're an active-duty military person, right away you're gonna be flagged as "Why are you applying for permanent residency in Canada? And you're active-duty military?" It was impossible to do that. So applying for refugee status was one way that a person could gain some kind of temporary status while the refugee claim was going through. The problem, of course, just in terms of how people generally see it, is "How can you be a refugee from the United States, our biggest trading partner?" And so it posed all kinds of questions in terms of refugee law.

In the *UN Handbook on Procedures and Criteria for Determining Refugee Status*, I think it's paragraph 171 says that if the war that you do not want to participate in is condemned by the international community as contrary to basic norms of human conduct, you might be considered a legitimate refugee claimant. Well, from the point of view of masses of Canadians, the war in Iraq was clearly an illegal war. It had no UN approval. The Security Council did not approve it. And just on a very basic moral basis, there were no weapons of mass destruction. It was a war of aggression. So we felt there was definitely a basis there—but obviously we're not lawyers! So that's when we really thought about the two tracks of this campaign—

a legal track, and a political track. While refugee claims are going forward, we campaign for a provision to be made to allow war resisters to stay. We don't care what the provision is—it can be a regulation, it can be a law, it can be a motion passed in Parliament. But the will of Canadians is that you make this happen—allow these Iraq War resisters to stay in Canada. And so that was the political campaign that we began.

On the legal front, the first case that went before the Immigration and Refugee Board was Jeremy Hinzman's case. And the federal government (a Liberal government) intervened to say that the question of the illegality of the Iraq War could not be raised as part of Jeremy's case for why he should be given refugee status. Right there, that took away a huge part of an argument that would have supported his claim for refugee status. And I think why the government did that is the legacy of the Vietnam War. They knew very well that a war like the one in Iraq, which was producing horrendous barbarism—if you think about Abu Ghraib, the use of white phosphorous, the massacres of people—was also producing resistance in the US military. And they could see down the line that they didn't want to allow that to go forward, with US soldiers coming to Canada. Canadian soldiers were in Afghanistan. For all intents and purposes, the Afghan and Iraq wars were one war. It's the "global war on terror." And so you can see the intersection of the Canadian military and the US military in this conflict. And I think it was just a calculation of theirs that they were going to nip this in the bud if they could.

But there were other avenues, legally, that developed in the course of this. As people's refugee claims were turned down, there were appeals. There were different layers of legal challenges that went forward. And those produced interesting results. And I think what it shows is that the intersection and interplay of the legal and political struggles is what allowed the fight to continue for 14 years to where we are today.

The resources of the Campaign were really whatever we could gather together in different rooms across the country. And so a lot of what we were able to provide to help people was based randomly on who was there at the table. Luckily, we had a number of people who had a background in social work or mental health, or health care generally, who were able to provide assistance that the Canadian state did not provide to resisters as refugee claimants. But again, it revealed these giant voids, these lacunae in social services for refugee claimants. And that was also a bit of a wakeup call for some of us who might not have been as intimately acquainted with the conditions that were facing refugee claimants in this country.

And the difficulty is that we were not a social service, we were a political campaign. So there were times we just didn't know what we could do. But by far the best resource to help war resisters I think, in that period, were other war resisters and other veterans. The connection with Iraq Veterans Against the War, with Vietnam veterans in the US who were in the field of psychiatry and so on, who were able to provide resources by Skype and things like that. We were able to get assistance to get a service dog in one situation for one of the war resisters who really couldn't function and leave the house without that. But our expertise didn't lie in that, and it was a definite learning curve.

One of the things that stood out quickly, as we began this campaign, was the degree to which opponents of Iraq War resisters tried to utilize the fact that there was no draft in the United States to undermine the legitimacy of Iraq War resisters' claims to asylum and access to safe haven.

The Canadian government, in particular under [Stephen] Harper when the Conservative Party won the election, attempted to not just make arguments like "US war resisters are bogus refugee claimants," but they also literally took down a website, a part of the website of the Immigration Department, that talked about the history of Vietnam War resisters. They literally deleted it. And that website showed that draft resisters and deserters from the US military were welcomed to Canada during the Vietnam War. So it was there for anybody to see, right on the website. Under then Minister of Immigration Jason Kenney's watch, that was removed. Subsequently, I think it was reinstated. But that was part of the campaign to erase the history of the Vietnam War resisters in Canada. That really struck a lot of campaigners: the importance of what we were doing in keeping that memory alive and keeping that gain that was made during the Vietnam War alive, in the face of the state literally erasing stuff from the historical record. So I think the fact that we were able to do that and to force them to reinstate it is important. Because we know that history matters, and knowing our history really matters.

We kept organizing to stop the deportations until the election in October 2015, when the Conservatives were kicked out. And since then it's been sort of a wait-and-see type of situation. But the fact that we were able to keep most people in until that election—the campaign strategy was: we must outlive the Tories. Not that we thought anyone else would naturally change direction, but at least there would be an opportunity for a new set of arguments to be deployed. If we could just last until that election, we might be able to find a solution.

There was a sense of joy at seeing the backside of the heinous Harper Government. I think in the Campaign from coast to coast, and in many campaigns—not just in the War Resisters Campaign—the sense of relief at not having the Harper-Kenney regime in power was palpable everywhere. But I think it was also clear to everyone that even with a change in government, the terrain had changed so dramatically in this country. Over the course of the 15 years of the Campaign, the degree of militarism, the degree of Canada's involvement in these military adventures, the sense that Canada was much meaner in terms of its immigration and refugee policies, a much harsher environment in terms of all kinds of social programs and so on, meant that we knew we were in for an ongoing challenge. No one had any illusions about that.

» When you're pulling together a campaign, you're just looking for anybody who can bring some expertise and some energy and enthusiasm to what you're trying to do. You're not really thinking about categories that people are in. One of the things we discovered is that there were a lot of women who were Vietnam War resisters, and who are still very much involved in different areas of politics and activism. So they got involved. I don't know what accounts for the particular role of women in this campaign, but it's clear right across the country. We put out the word that we wanted to establish committees and campaigns in different cities to welcome war resisters, because at a certain point in Toronto we started to be overwhelmed with the number of people and we didn't have enough housing. We didn't have enough resources locally. Often, it was women who established those committees. Many of them were already involved in peace activities. But others had been involved during the Vietnam War and opened their homes. That's not to say there weren't also men, but it was interesting there was a leadership role of women right across the country in the Campaign.

Pretty soon we also discovered that there was also a funny commonality amongst campaigners in Toronto: a lot of us were LGBTQ individuals. It just seemed like, "Oh, interesting coincidence." But it was pretty noticeable in the Toronto campaign in particular. The mainstays were the same people throughout almost the entire 14-year history of the Campaign. And a good chunk of those, not representative of the percentage in Canadian population, were LGBTQ people. I've thought about it a number of times. And the only thing I can think of is that just on a visceral level, being denied bodily autonomy, being denied the right to do what you want with your body, including being killed for a war you don't believe in, is fundamental to the struggle for LGBTQ liberation. It's just fundamental to what we're fighting for. That's the intersection I see. But there might be other, more interesting explanations.

The fact that people who are gay or lesbian or trans or whatever decide to get involved in this campaign doesn't mean they've all had necessarily a very similar activism previously. But just dealing with life as an LGBTQ person can provide that basic sympathy, I think.

The political challenges and legal obstacles were huge. The political context was very different in 2004 than in 1969. But what hadn't changed was the degree of popular support for allowing war resisters to stay in Canada. From what I understand between the Vietnam War and the Iraq War, it's the same number that supports: two-thirds of Canadians, 64 percent, wanted Iraq War resisters to be allowed to stay in Canada. We had two motions passed in Parliament to allow Iraq War resisters to stay in Canada.

One thing that's kept the Campaign very much afloat throughout this whole period is that we know the war resisters. We know their stories. Every time they speak about what they've experienced and why they walked away from the war and what it cost them and why they came here and what it's meant for them to be here and to be working with us—that's a main reason people keep going. The other is that the vast majority agree with us. So that keeps you going. And I think that we will win this ultimately.

I think one of the things that we've been able to do through the Vietnam War resisters, and the Iraq War resisters, through both of those experiences, is to ground the whole issue in what is happening at the receiving end of these wars. That's a lesson that I hope will carry forward: the voices of the Vietnamese who were being bombed by the American forces in Vietnam, the stories of the Iraqis and their resistance to occupation and the invasion by the US-led forces. We really try to bring those voices forward, partly through war resisters just telling their stories. And also by connecting with communities here who had that link with the people on the receiving end of the war. That's one of the things I hope could be a useful contribution to future movements that try to extend this kind of solidarity.

Corey just before he left the US for Canada. (Photo courtesy of Corey.)

10 Corey

I WAS BORN IN INDIANA IN 1982. I lived in a very flat, very small, boring town.

I'd almost been convinced to enlist while in high school by recruiters. Then my older sister joined the National Guard some years later to pay for university. She talked me into talking to a recruiter. I was 19. I wanted to have a discussion with him about joining the National Guard. The reason for not going fully into the military was because I didn't want to go live on a base or have to go to war, unless there were troops invading America. She explained, "The National Guard, they don't do that; they're there for home defence."

I went to talk to the recruiter. He assured me that the National Guard doesn't go to foreign countries; we don't fight wars on foreign soil. It's like the Minutemen in the Revolutionary War. I ended up signing up. I needed to get a job and go back to school. We'd get floods and tornadoes in Indiana. The National Guard comes out, helps pick stuff up. It's kind of cool. I would do that anyway, so why not get paid for it and go to school for free? So, yes, I'll do that. Everything was as planned for the first few years.

I signed up in 2002. It was one weekend a month, two weeks a year. I flew through basic training, nine weeks, and then went to advanced training, which was like college-level courses, and did that for six or eight months. Basically, you were playing army for the first part of the day, going to school for the last part. I did a lot of schooling because they told me I'd earn college credits for time in these classes. Then I came back home after a few months and worked at a recruit training detachment. I got side jobs with the Guard occasionally. I worked at a cable company for a while, then I would play army on the weekends once a month and two weeks in the summer. It was like that for three years or so.

Then we got orders to deploy to Iraq in support of Operation Iraqi Freedom. That would've been around 2005. They were talking about sending National Guard all over the place, so I started getting a little wary of what I had done. They were jerking me around on going to school, not wanting to pay for it. So I ended up paying for my own schooling. Shortly after I got activated, I went AWOL a couple of times.

I'd been lied to about the whole "We don't go to foreign wars" thing. I didn't sign up for that. I went AWOL twice. The first time I got promoted, and the second time I got jailed for eight days and demoted three grades. At that point, I'd already missed the deployment. I didn't want to be in the National Guard. I'd never been to jail and had never really been in trouble. I didn't sign up for the Guard to be on probation. Some admin guy at the armoury said I should transfer units. All this company-level stuff goes away when you transfer states.

I'm like, okay, I'll transfer units, maybe I'll go try to live in California. I thought, California's pretty liberal, they aren't going to send people to Iraq. So I moved to California. I thought I would just camp it out and see where it goes, and find a job. I was there for a couple of weeks, staying on the beaches, homeless. Eventually, I did find a job and hooked up with the National Guard, had my file transferred. When they transferred my file, the demotion was just a physical demotion, not a paper demotion. I thought I'd take it seriously again. I did really well at first. They got me into a really good unit. Everything was cool. I didn't have a place to live at the time, so they let me stay in the armoury till I found a place. They got me lined up to go to military intelligence school, and I had this grand plan of going to school to ride out the last years of my contract. I'm not re-enlisting, just getting a lot of college credits, and then transferring those credits over and going to school: go for a year or two to get a degree in something, get a better job, and completely be done with the military.

So I thought I'd ride this out. Then I got orders again to go to Iraq. I mean, I spent time in jail for not going the last time. So I thought, just grind out the deployment: 18 months in a tactical operation centre on a base. That was the gig. First they had me just filling the slot of a radio operator, which is the lowest thing I trained to do. This would be fine.

In training leading up to the deployment, we practised kicking in doors, cordon and searching, and doing convoys. And I was like, man, this is not what I thought we were going to do.

We had to do this training before going to Iraq. Everybody was always trying to pull me to their section for some reason. The S3/S2 shop had the most pull because they're operations and intel—they pulled me in as a Battle [Staff] NCO [non-commissioned officer] and the MI [military intelligence] analyst for the swing shift. They had promoted me to sergeant during this training phase.

I'd been promoted to E-5 sergeant and given charge of two soldiers. Then we go into a train-up in Germany, outside Nuremberg. That's where I found out just following orders is not an excuse. Which was the only reason I was there. I thought, Well, maybe we aren't being told everything that's going on there. You know, maybe there's more going on than we know. Plus, there's a lot of propaganda supporting the war on TV at that point.

After Germany, I came back to Texas to finish training. Upon arrival we received a weekend pass. I decided 18 months was a long time, and I'd heard really bad stories about the place we were going. They called it Mortaritaville, 'cause it got mortared every day. I didn't want a mushy goodbye from the family, so I went to Vegas instead and blew all the money that I made in training.

Finally I was in Iraq as this swing-shift MI analyst and Battle NCO. As part of the job, you're in charge of the operations centre along with the Battle Captain, making sure everybody turns in their reports for water, where supplies are going, and then documenting everything that happens in the theatre of the war.

Also, I was in charge of "extra duty." There were about 20 people that I would have to put to work, doing area beautification or random tasks. I'd have them sweep the floors or make gardens or whatever I could think of, make them clean or take out all the lights and clean off the bulbs. Dumb stuff. Sometimes I would just have to make up things to keep them busy. I hated it. I didn't like punishing people.

So I made a deal. I talked to my commanders and arranged a deal. If these guys do online courses—show me they're doing the courses, or come here to do them, I'll have them do those instead of just sitting around cleaning things every day. Still have them clean, but after, they can do this. They're going to be screwed after Iraq. Many of them had been demoted in Iraq and they're just keeping them around to fill boots. When they get back to the States, they're going to get kicked out of the Guard. I did hear some of them did some really bad things, but I was fair and offered the same thing to everybody.

Anyway, I'd have to coordinate with our upper headquarters stuff that had happened in the theatre. There was more coming up in the news: no weapons of mass destruction and such. There were a lot of really bad things going on that I can't really discuss happening there as well, with how we were handling things, and how they were being reported. I was getting flak for trying to question things: like, this doesn't tell me what's going on. This doesn't really seem like it makes sense. When I would question it, the response would be: "Yo, stay in your lane, man, and you just report the data." Part of the job was taking the sitrep (situation report) and then making a story of that, like raw data. I would have to take that data and write a story. You just had this raw data and created something like: so we're driving down this road, they took fire from four enemy blah blah blah. Some of these sitreps, they weren't adding up, and things are missing in the timeline. So I eventually didn't want any part of it. And mainly there were no weapons of mass destruction, which was the only reason I had that justified going in the first place.

I knew it all along. We weren't supposed to be in Iraq. This was all just a ploy. This was all made up to get us here. I tried to give two weeks' notice, like a resignation letter, and the top wouldn't accept it. They told me I was just "stressed out," and they'd send me home on leave in two weeks. I said, "Okay. That's cool. I just won't come back after that." And they're like, "Oh, no, you'll be back because desertion during wartime is punishable by death. If you keep talking like that, we won't let you leave." Afterwards, I thought that I was really stupid. I should've just said okay to the two weeks.

A few days later they are like, "Hey, I got that leave for you. You know, I hope you had a chance to think about our conversation, and we'll see you back here in two weeks when you're fresh and relaxed." I said, "Okay, sorry about that." And I went home, back to Indiana, and saw my parents.

I leave things to chance sometimes. This time I decided to leave it up to the alarm for the day I was supposed to return. I left my phone, one of those flip phones back then. I didn't set an alarm to wake up for my flight. I thought, If I wake up in time to go, I'd go back. But if I don't, then I'm not going.

I had a girlfriend in Indiana who was very supportive of me leaving the army any way I could. She said, "If you do it, you're welcome to stay here. Then we figure out what to do." So I slept in and didn't wake up for the flight. The military didn't have any of her information, but they had my parents' information. They didn't have any data on my whereabouts though. I threw away my phone. I don't think I had a computer or anything like that. So I just hung out, went to concerts...I had some money saved up. I lived off of that for a while, got little jobs where I could.

I eventually left her because I thought I was going to get her in trouble. It was too difficult to tell her that I was going...She would've tried to convince me out of it. So I left without saying anything. From then I was hanging out at my friends' houses, couch-surfing from place to place, staying in college dorms, because all my friends were at school. I was really concerned about becoming an annoyance or a burden, so I never really stayed anywhere too long.

Eventually, I thought I couldn't be the only person who did this. I went to the library, googled or yahoo'd—maybe Asked Jeeves, not sure—anyway, I looked up "desertion" and found out that during Vietnam, people went to Canada. I ran across a news article about a person who left the army due to an Iraq deployment and went to Canada. I found out who their lawyer was, went to a pay phone, and called him up.

The lawyer gave me another number to the Campaign office, which I called next. They said they can't make any promises—basically, "If you end up here, we'll see if we can help." I didn't know what the border would be like. I had these two friends—they drove me up. I'd spent at least a year hiding out in the States at that point.

We came to Canada for a day trip, crossed the border in Windsor. When the border guards searched the car, they found my checklist of things I needed to do when I came to Canada. And they're like, "What's this? Are you planning to stay here? If you're checking out living here at some point, here's a card with info. Contact CIC [Citizenship and Immigration Canada]. You can call them up and find out what you need to do."

I had no plans at this point. So they gave me literature on how to emigrate to Canada. I went to Toronto. I met with Lee and some members of the [War Resisters Support] Campaign.

I drove straight to Toronto from Windsor. This person, who's a photography teacher, offered their place up for two weeks. My friends stayed for a couple days. It's funny because I was completely broke at the time. I had 400 dollars when I came, and I had offered to pay for my driver's gas here, take them out for dinner and drinks, as well as gas money to get back. I should have 160 bucks left over. Their car got towed while out for dinner and drinks. I paid for their car to get out of tow, which was exactly 160 dollars. They left, and I was flat broke.

Luckily the Campaign set me up with this place I could stay. Back then, rent was cheap. New people would show up nearly every day. I would let them stay, if I had room, till they found a place to stay.

A lot of them didn't stay. It was too difficult. They stayed for a few months and they would go back because they missed their families or whatever. Things were good for a while. Everything was pretty stable. I had landed a job and was thinking about trying to go back to school. Then they tried to deport me a couple times.

My claim was rejected in 2008 or 2009—I don't do so well with dates. It's been a while. I was getting deported. My plan was to catch a plane to Amsterdam. No one had done the research at that point on where to go if it didn't work out here. I thought Amsterdam probably seemed like it would be the easiest place for me to go. I had some friends there.

Then as I was getting up to get on the plane, my lawyer called and said, "Don't get on the plane. They rescinded the deportation order and you got an appeal." I had sold everything I owned. I quit my job and got rid of my apartment. I had nowhere to go. Just had a backpack of stuff that I planned on bringing with me to Amsterdam. My friend was in Amsterdam waiting for me.

Eventually, I found a place to stay, and then I was almost deported again. A few weeks after that, it happened a third time. The third time, they tried to deport, like, five of us at the same time.

I thought, Somebody's got to start doing groundwork. If anybody could try, I could probably figure out a way to do it. And if not, I was getting tossed out anyway so it didn't matter. I talked to some members of the Campaign, and they said they would support me if I wanted to do this. We talked about other options. We talked about sanctuary, about the future. But leaving seemed like the best way, because another person was already in sanctuary in Europe. It had been years, and it seemed like that was going nowhere. We didn't know what was going to happen politically. So I decided to catch a flight to Ireland.

The Campaign had some contacts, people that could at least help out for getting situated. So I got there, lined up everything, got a lawyer. I thought, you know, like, This is only the first stop. I shouldn't just jump right into this. I should see if there is another option.

I thought I'd check out some other places to see if Ireland is the best option. I was in Dublin, stayed in Ireland for quite a bit. I ended up having a few places I could crash there. Then I was doing this thing called HelpX, which was volunteering in return for room and board. I ended up staying all over the place. I can only be in Ireland for three months at a time on a visitor visa. I decided to go to Europe, where I could stay for three months. I thought, Okay, I'll get it out of the way now, since I know I can be in Ireland, but maybe there's a better option where it isn't going to be such a big deal to stay.

I thought, I'll go to Amsterdam, see what's going on there. And I lined up some places in Europe to HelpX. So I did that and ended up in Amsterdam. I linked up with this other friend. We were on a boat, sailing the canals. We were going to go to London from there. I thought, Okay, I'll get some of Europe, at least Amsterdam, out of the way. Head to London and see if there's any options there. I had done a lot of online research at that point, but still, maybe I can figure out something else. Or maybe just lie low. London should be an easy place to do that. I don't know why I thought that about London, having never been there, but it didn't matter because the mast broke on the boat, and we couldn't very easily "sail the English Channel" without that. We could have motored over, but it didn't have the same appeal I guess, and it was going to end up costing me to get across. So I got off in Rotterdam. I thought, Okay, well, what am I going to do now?

After a few days in Rotterdam, I checked in with the Campaign. This reporter was doing a story on the guy who had filed a claim for asylum in Germany. He was interested in meeting up with me and offered to let me tag along. I thought, It would be nice to figure out what is going on there. So the reporter picked me up in Rotterdam. He said he had a few places he wanted to go while there, and I was welcome to come along for the ride and he would drop me off wherever I wanted after we went to Germany to do the interview. The interview was in two weeks. We went through a few countries, did some sightseeing, and visited people he'd done a story on before. After that adventure I ended up having the reporter drop me off in Frankfurt, Germany. I hung out there for a while. I had a friend who worked on an army base. Him and I went to high school together. He said, "Crash at my place." I stayed there for a little bit and then remembered that I'd worked on a film once, and the sound dude told me if I ever ran into problems staying in Canada, make it to Europe, then give him a call. He was in Berlin, Germany.

I called him up, "Hey, man, I'm in Germany. You said to call." So he's like, "Oh yeah, dude, let's meet up for a beer."

The German dude ended up having a child with the person who lives next door to him in their apartment building. So they had both apartments and a spare bedroom. I was able to stay in the spare room, but my visa was almost running out at that point to stay in Europe. We stumbled onto this Berlin freelance artist visa scheme. At that point I was just on a Schengen visitor's visa, which is three months. So I had two options: I could go to Turkey for six months on a visitor visa or I could go to England for six months. Either one would reset my Schengen and Irish visitor visas. I had a gig lined up in London, and then the conscientious objectors' movement in Turkey said they'd put me up, which was like the war resister international campaign. I didn't know anything about it. So I thought I'd find out more about this. Maybe there are some options in Turkey. I had no idea about the political circumstances there at that point. I knew a little bit, but not a lot. So I decided, Okay, now I can go on to Istanbul. So the plan was my buddy would do the legwork on getting a freelance visa in Germany. When I come back, we work on the visa. He's going to round up cash, because I need 10,000 euros. I needed to show

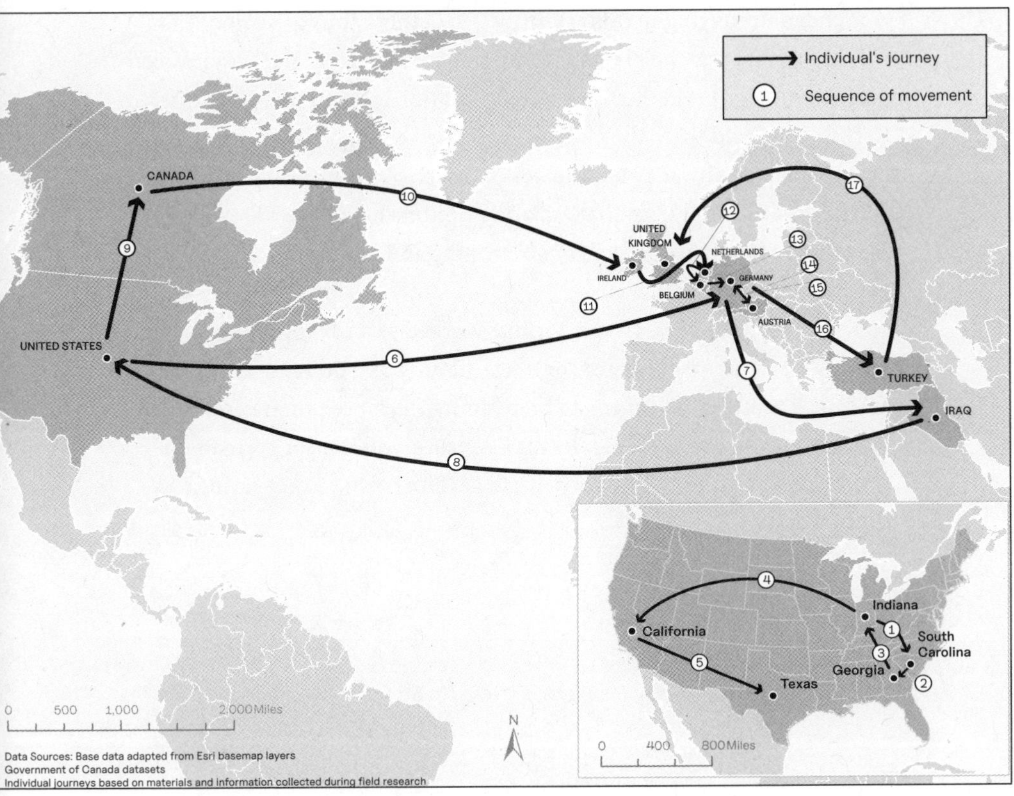

MAP 4: Corey's journey from 2005 to the 2010s.

that I had it in the bank. He said, "All right, I'll figure out a way to loan you the money to put into your bank account."

So I went to Istanbul, Turkey. Met with the international war resisters league of conscientious objectors. They're all Kurdish for the most part. They have conscription in Turkey. Resisters there are not in the military because they'd be forced to fight other Kurdish people, based on what they had told me. They explained the Kurds are being put down there in an almost genocidal way. I hung out with them for a while. I had a job teaching English there at the time. It got a little dangerous politically. So I remembered I had another option still in Scotland for a place to stay. So I left before the six-month visa expired.

I ended up staying in this castle for, like, I think four or six months, helping out around the place for room and board. The sir and the lady were nice. Eventually, I told them about the situation I was in. They had offered to help, but I told them they had really helped enough already. After that I eventually made my way back to Berlin. I had to make this Berlin thing work because, other than that, no other options looked good long-term. Travelling around every three or six months and not having a home is exhausting.

So I eventually got a visa in Berlin. I worked as a photographer and a writer. I got a job working for the news, filming and doing sound. I was able to be completely legitimate there doing freelance camera and sound work. After you live there legally for five years, you can get permanent residence. Then after ten years you can get citizenship. Long-term, it could work.

Professional photograph of John taken in Montreal around 2018. (Photo courtesy of John.)

11 John F.

I WAS BORN IN 1946 and raised in Brooklyn, New York. My parents were your classic WW II veteran couple. Fortunately for me, my family had been in the States for a few generations, so I had the advantage of at least two or three generations of education in English preceding me. So I had a head start in school, and I was always a star student. I'm in the same age cohort almost precisely with Bill Clinton, George W. Bush, and, unfortunately, Donald Trump.

I was in that group of white boys my age who were supposed leaders of tomorrow. At least that's what Disney told us on TV. I have one sister, only a year and a half younger. She had the same advantages that I did, except for one thing: she was a woman. When we were kids, we were still fully in the male supremacy world. So the smartest girls were the smartest girls, but the future winners were going to be the smartest boys. So I had all those advantages and sailed through school.

I went to St. John's University, which then had a location in Brooklyn. In my third year at St. John's, 31 young university instructors there were turfed. It was a unionization effort that was dealt with by dumping the non-tenured young instructors involved. That triggered me off. The next thing you know, I was a leader in a student strike at St. John's in 1966. The strike utterly failed without enough faculty or student support. I didn't have to go back to St. John's with my tail between my legs because New York University (NYU) offered any third-year student the opportunity to transfer with full credit.

Why was it important that I have an immediate academic refuge? Because of the draft. I was riding on a succession of student draft deferments. If I had not remained a full-time university student, I would have been drafted. But because NYU took me in on virtually no notice, I didn't miss a beat. So I graduated from NYU rather than from St. John's in 1967. I was only 21, so I still had five years of draft exposure as the draft was then set up.

As soon as I got to NYU undergraduate, I finally started thinking: I've only got a year and a half left for this BA; then I need five more years of a draft deferment. What am I going to do? Oh, law school. That's three years. So I went to the pre-law advisor at NYU. I explained, "I'm going to be only 21 when I graduate in 1967. I need five more years of draft deferment. Law school is three years. Where are the fattest scholarships in the country to law school? I have no money, so I need three years of a fat scholarship. How do I get one?" So he looks at me and he says, "Frankly, you're not properly motivated. You know, you're supposed to know why you want to go to law school." (I knew why I wanted to go to law school: that's three more years of draft deferment. I just don't have any money.) He brushed me off.

Fortunately, I did very well on the Law School Admission Test (the LSAT). When I went back to the pre-law advisor at NYU, he had just received the latest LSAT results. His face says, Why didn't you tell me you were smart?! Now he tells me that the best law school scholarship in the country is right here at NYU. I got all of the application materials. I applied for this scholarship, which was then known as the Root-Tilden Scholarship, named after two famous NYU Law alumni. I won one. (Open to men only as of 1967; we were still in the dark ages. None of the smart women could compete for that scholarship. I mean, young people today may or may not realize just how recent this male supremacy was.) So, poof: three more years of draft deferment. I started NYU Law in '67.

End of January 1968: Tet Offensive. The Communists in Vietnam rose up at the Tet holiday, late January 1968, and although this massive uprising was, in due course, suppressed by Uncle Sam, assisted by the South Vietnamese forces, that was the end of the credibility of the Vietnam War from the American point of view. No one had thought that the Communist side was still capable of wreaking this much havoc. We'd been told for years: "It's getting better, it will be over soon." So even though the Tet Offensive was militarily not a success for the Communists, it was a decisive psychological victory. That was the end of believing, "It's almost over. It's going to be all right."

President Johnson and his regime reacted by doing something that, I must admit, was "fair." As this war was not going to end any time soon, it was no longer tenable that all these boys on student draft deferments could permanently avoid service. So this marked the end of graduate student deferments, except for medical, dental, and clerical. All other male post-baccalaureate students: you're losing your deferment with the stroke of a pen on Friday, February 16, 1968. Black Friday it was called by many of us. That was the announcement of the end of most graduate student deferments. So here I was, halfway through the first year of law. I was supposed to be there for three years. Now I have to scramble. So then followed a musical-chairs type situation: graduate students, graduating BA students, scrambling for a smaller number of draft deferment or draft exempt spots.

I should have been able to get one of those spots, because one of those spots was elementary or high school teacher. Anyway, I didn't move fast enough, and I was exposed to immediate induction. However, I was able to delay actually being drafted for a little over one more year. You had an automatic right of appeal if you had been classified as eligible for immediate induction. So I appealed. I didn't have any grounds that they were going to accept. But the process itself took time, and they were not drafting you in the middle of an academic semester. So it toppled forward to the end of my second year at NYU Law. I was able to log two years at NYU Law. Then I finally got drafted. I was inducted into the US Army at Fort Hamilton, Brooklyn, New York, on Wednesday, July 16, 1969.

Why do I have such a vibrant, really good memory of my induction date? On that day, Apollo 11 blasted off. This was going to be the first humans landing on the moon. Friday, July 18, the spacecraft is still heading to the moon. The Chappaquiddick incident, Ted Kennedy. Senator Ted Kennedy supposedly drives off a bridge after a party and a young woman in his car ends up dead. And then Monday, July 21, I've now been in the Army for four or five days: "You men, there'll be no processing today because we landed on the moon yesterday. The President has called a holiday today."

They put me in the infantry. I found out later that they liked university graduates in the infantry because if the lieutenant and the sergeant get killed, somebody has to take over the platoon. And the 23-year-old university graduate is going to be looked up to by the 19-year-old draftees. I experienced that in training.

So infantry, and then towards the very end of our AIT [advanced infantry training], we were given our orders on paper in black and white: RVN, Republic of Vietnam, Eleven B, meaning infantry. And then they gave us a three-week leave of absence to go home and say goodbye. So I got to New York at the beginning of that three weeks.

My father and his buddies were shocked that they would give me upfront notice of my orders. In WW II, they were given a weekend off and then told to report to the railroad station. They weren't told where they were going next. I thought, Are they pointing out an aspect of this that I hadn't thought of? I do have advance knowledge. I have three weeks. Let's try something.

I didn't know how to handle it. So I went down to Washington, DC, and tried to see my congressman. That got nowhere. What I should have done was to go down to the Pentagon, or to a bar near the Pentagon, and try to talk to somebody, or something like that. But I was only 23, and I was sort of in distress—shock, if you will. I wasn't able to do anything to change anything within the system.

Most of my classmates at NYU Law were still in their third year of law. They threw a party for me during those three weeks I was back in New York, and the place was packed. They all had their worried faces. One of them takes me by the shoulders. This was a young veteran of the Black civil rights movement in the South. He takes me by the shoulders and says, "I hear you're ordered to 'Nam. Yeah? Well, you're not going, are ya?" And I thought, Well, I do have a decision here...

I started looking into Canada right away. The anti-war people in New York—and I don't remember what they were called. They were affiliated, I think, with the Quakers—they had an office in New York. I went to see them. They told me up front, "As you may imagine, everything we say is being recorded by the US government. As you may imagine, we are not allowed to counsel any breaking of any law." So I thought, Okay, that means please ask your questions circumspectly. So instead of them counselling me to do anything, I asked factual questions. And they gave neutral factual answers, in a sequence such as, "Do you have any knowledge about young American men in my situation seeking immigrant status in Canada?"

"We have heard of that."

It quickly became clear to me. University graduate, age 18 to 39, good health, fluent in English, partial law school, no criminal record: come on in, 50 Canada Immigration points.

» So on the day that I was supposed to fly from New York to the state of Washington to report at Fort Lewis for transshipment to Vietnam, instead of going to Washington state I went to Montreal by plane. Somehow I was told, "Do not take a bus. The bus is the cheapest. Therefore, they assume that the dodgers and deserters will likely be on a bus." So a plane in those days, I don't know the inflation factor, but I think it was about 60 bucks, New York to Montreal. At the beginning of the three-week leave of absence, the Army gave us a bunch of cash, which was supposed to pay to go home, say goodbye, and then go to Washington state. So I had the 60 dollars.

I also had about 900 dollars in a savings account, which I emptied out. So I armed myself with 900 dollars in US fund traveller's cheques and my remaining cash from what Uncle Sam had just given me, and came to Canada by plane.

I had been to Expo 67 as a tourist with a bunch of Brooklyn university students. The only thing I knew about Canada was Montreal. I'd been in Montreal for about a week. I thought Montreal was a great town.

So I flew to Montreal, and I'd been told by the anti-war people that an American citizen aged 18 to 39 could just ask outright to be processed as an immigrant. I was 23. I did. "Fine, come this way." I looked like all the other young men on the plane that morning. They were all fit young businessmen. Young men with small briefcases who were delivering papers and certified cheques. I looked just like them, except for two things: I was in slightly better physical shape than they were, and I had shorter hair than they did, although not that much shorter. I mean, they had short hair because that's what Wall Street wanted. I fit right in.

I had a small suitcase, so it's slightly bigger than their briefcases. And they were all saying the same thing to the nodding Customs guy at the first spot. He was asking, "Purpose of trip?" Then they would each answer,

"Business." "Length of stay?" "One day." Then it came to me. "Purpose of trip?" "Immigration." "Length of stay?" "Lifetime." "Oh, you go over here." So then I went to the Canada Immigration Office at Dorval Airport, as it then was, before it became the Pierre Elliott Trudeau Airport. I filled out a form, and where it said "Record of Employment," I deliberately put as the most recent employment "US Army; job, draftee." I wanted to get it on the record. No, I thought, I'm not going to get in trouble with the government of Canada. Tell the truth. So I was ushered in to speak to a young French Canadian guy. I pointed with my finger to the spot where I'd written "US Army, draftee." I said, "What about this?" He said, "Oh, Mr. F__, please. That is an American problem."

I knew from that moment that it was going to be all right. He pulls out a sheet of paper, which turns out to be a temporary work permit. He says that it will take eight to ten weeks to process the application to be a landed immigrant. "But the only reason why we have to delay it is because we have to check the veracity of what you've told us. But of course, you have told us the truth. Everything will be fine. During that time, here is a temporary work permit." WHAP! He slaps on the date stamp. "You can go anywhere in Canada, work, get a social insurance number. Just keep me abreast of your address so I can send you in the mail your landed immigrant card when it's ready." So I'm sitting there, and I'm holding this paper.

He was probably used to the shocked but happy look that must have been on my face.

He rises up. He sticks out his hand. He says, "Bienvenue au Canada!" For all intents and purposes, I'm an immigrant to Canada. I look at my watch. My plane took off three hours ago at whatever airport I went to in Queens, New York. Three hours later, I'm in.

» I had not told my parents of my plan to take off for Canada. My father needed an ex post facto fait accompli. He could never have coped knowing that I was planning to leave the USA. And since I couldn't tell him, I didn't want to implicate my mother and create a rift between them. Even though there was no danger in me telling my mother, I was right in not having done so. My mother, though, was 100 percent favourable to my having absconded to Canada, when she learned that I had.

I called my parents and sister that evening from an airport motel just outside Dorval Airport. My mother and sister were completely supportive. My father, on the other hand, was a basket case for a good while. He didn't know how to cope. However, within two years he was on my side, because during those two years, all the revelations about the Vietnam War had started to come out. By 1972, he was completely reconciled. "Thank God my son didn't go."

Six months after I moved to Canada, after I had settled in Toronto, to which I'd by then moved from Montreal, my father drove up with a carload of my stuff. Even though we were not yet fully reconciled, he never disowned me, never refused to speak to me. He was just upset and puzzled. Even though he was in that state, he drove up.

I think my mother and sister probably sorted which of my items was important memorabilia, which were to be thrown away, and whatnot. So by June of 1970, six months after I deserted, I had all my vital stuff.

» That first night, Friday, December 12, 1969, at the airport motel in Dorval, I just cried myself to sleep. Second day, okay. So from Saturday, December 13, 1969, I started trying to find a place to live and get a job. I had one phone number in Montreal to call. This was a friend of one of my NYU Law classmates. The guy was the same age I was and a medical student or resident. So on the Saturday, I called him and his young wife, newlyweds. They lived in an apartment building near the campus of McGill University. So they invited me to their home. We had dinner at their home on the Saturday, and then they took me to a rooming house on Pine Avenue West in Montreal, surrounded by McGill. I got a room for 18 dollars a week. It was a decent room, shared bathroom down the hall, big kitchen, and it was all students.

I would go out on the business days looking for work. I remember I was in tip-top physical condition. I was 23 years old, straight out of 16 or 17 weeks of physical training. In the mornings, I would eat my little bowl of cereal or whatever I provided for myself for breakfast. And then I would put on my one suit, my one tie. I think I probably had two or three white shirts. I would walk down the steps of Montreal to the downtown business district and look for work, and then walk back up to my rooming house at day's end. I was trying to market myself as a rookie bank manager trainee type because my summer job, from late university through NYU Law, had been bank teller.

I was in Montreal just a few days, and here comes Christmas, December of '69. I found out, probably from the peace movement, about the American Deserters Committee. I ended up going to a Christmas dinner at their Montreal office. And there I met a bunch of guys, of course, recent arrivals like me. But it quickly became evident to me that these guys mostly just wanted to go back to the US. They were longing to go back. They were longing to have influence on what was going on in the States.

My headspace was that it's going to be many years before I can ever go back. By that time, it's going back as a visitor. I'm not going to do jail. Therefore, I'm not going to go back until jail is off the table. I have to accept the fact that I'm going to be a Canadian. And these poor guys, though they had status here, were still yearning to go back to the States.

I felt sorry for these guys, but I couldn't pretend that I agreed with how they were planning to handle this very difficult time. They weren't happy to be here. I did go back to their office, but not more than two or three times, because I could see that they wanted to talk, not about how we were doing in being brand-new Canadians, but about how we could try to change what was going on in the US.

» I was in Montreal, a bilingual city, but one in which French was the predominant language. I was not capable of working in French. I did have a weak rudimentary French as an Anglo junior high, high school, and university student, but it was not nearly enough to use at work. After two months, by mid-February 1970, I knew enough to realize that, as essentially a unilingual Anglo, I should be in Toronto. I had picked the wrong city. (But psychologically, Montreal had been the right initial choice. I'd had to go to something that I "knew.")

I stayed in Montreal for two months, and then I moved to Toronto.

I arrived in Toronto by bus just before midnight on Friday, February 13, 1970. Why do I remember that date? Because I realized shortly thereafter that I'd chosen to make a big life move on Friday the 13th! I was oblivious to that when I was doing it.

So I get to Toronto at midnight by bus. Across the street from the bus terminal in those days was a hotel known as the Hotel Ford.

So I just got off the bus, walked across the street, and took a room at the Hotel Ford. It was seven dollars and change a night, including whatever taxes were involved—not bad. I couldn't afford seven dollars a night for any length of time, so I needed a room in a rooming house. I paid 11 dollars a week for a furnished little room in Cabbagetown (where there were then many rooming houses), which I found the next day.

Fortunately for me, there was, a little over a month after my arrival in Toronto, an ad in the *Globe and Mail* "Help Wanted" pages, which seemed to be aimed at someone just like me. In those days, "Help Wanted Male" and "Help Wanted Female" were listed separately. This was handy for a guy, because you only had to look at the male listing. But of course it was revealing, how the job descriptions in the two different listings showed the dichotomy of how men and women had to cope with the job market in those days.

Before I landed the job described in that ad, I'd go out every business day looking for work. I was in the employment office of one of the banks I tried, and filled out their white application form or their yellow application form. One colour's form was for the men. The other colour's form was for the women, which was not unusual or surprising to a guy of my generation, not at all. That's the way the world was then. So I filled out the male application form and handed it in. Now I'm waiting for an interview. But I was curious what, apart from the fact that they're different colours, what was the actual difference in the two different application forms? I checked. There was only one question that was different. Male application form: "Are you willing to relocate anywhere in Canada?" Female application form: "Are you willing to work anywhere in Metropolitan Toronto?" (Male, management. Woman, underling.)

Back to the ad which led to my first job in Canada. I was reading the *Globe* one day, and there was an ad from the Guaranty Trust Company of Canada. They needed an "assistant trust officer." The requirements were "appropriate education and relevant experience." Well, they're casting the net, but not widely enough to include women in those days. This ad was in the "Help Wanted Male" section, and "man" was included in the wording of the ad. I found nothing unusual about that in those days. I answered the ad.

They liked me, they hired me. I started in mid-April. It took me two months in Montreal, a move to Toronto, and two months in Toronto. I now had a job.

But even after I got the job at Guaranty Trust and started being trained for eventual branch management, my personal life was pretty isolated, until a very good thing happened. At the six-month mark on the job, after I was finished with what amounted to boot camp for men at Guaranty Trust, I was ready to be sent out to the branches. "We want to send you to one of our biggest branches: Niagara Falls." I said, "You are aware that I cannot cross the border. I mean, do you really want to put me in a border town?"

"Well, your work won't have anything to do with the New York side. Just don't accidentally go off to play on the New York side."

So off I went to Niagara Falls. That was a terrific move for me because here I come to this small city, 65,000 (I don't think it's grown or shrunk since). This little old downtown Niagara Falls, the old business district. As soon as I got to that small workplace in a small town, that was the end of being isolated. Everybody there was like, "This nice young man doesn't know anybody. We're going to take him in." I stood out like a sore thumb on the street. "Who's that nice-looking young man in a suit and tie looking lonesome?" So from then on they forcefully took me in.

So I was incorporated into the small business community of Niagara Falls, Ontario. And I started to meet lawyers and law clerks and other people. One of them said to me, "Why don't you go back to law school?" I told them that I had no money and that I was a felon on the lam: an accused felon on the lam from the US. "Well, you forget about that. First of all, nobody gives a damn that you're a deserter. And number two, you Americans, you assume law school is as expensive up here as it is down there. Look into it. And by the way, we have Canada student loans and Ontario student awards. And you already have two years of law school. Go back to law." So I did.

I was given one year's credit for the two years I had done at NYU Law. So I was able to enter as a second-year law student in a three-year program, which was vital because that pole-vaulted me over all the applicants for first-year seats. I was accepted at Western, Queen's, and the University of Toronto, and I picked U of T. Although I was in Niagara Falls, I knew about Toronto. I loved Toronto. So, September of 1971, I shuffled from Guaranty Trust, Niagara Falls, Ontario, to the St. George Graduate Residence, Bloor and St. George, U of T.

I did two years of law at U of T. I lived at the St. George Graduate Residence, which no longer exists. So imagine, here's a guy, 25 years old, living in a building with 250 or more age-appropriate men and women, all looking for friendship, all singles looking for romance or friendship. Some of them were pining loners. I mean, some of them were total fish out of water. All they needed was a tiny number of residents to take charge of a social program. Well, guess who took charge?

For two years I was, assisted by my roommate and others, the de facto chairperson of the social committee. We had a lot of events, and a number of romances—the latter, unfortunately, not including me. Several couples that I introduced to each other or caused to be introduced. While I was meanwhile doing just enough work at school to pass and get my law degree.

At the St. George residence, who was my roommate my first year there? One of my fellow Irish Catholic New Yorkers, who was a Vietnam veteran. An anti-war Vietnam veteran, a member of VVAW (Vietnam Veterans Against the War). I don't know if people at the residence were conscious of the fact that there's a Vietnam veteran and a deserter living, in the same room, among them. He and I socialized together all the time. We were significant friends of each other for a few years, before we unfortunately drifted apart.

He was anti-war. He had enlisted. He became an intelligence officer. He lived with Vietnamese people. He was embedded in a town or village. He had a sidearm, and a Vietnamese girlfriend. A different experience from what I would likely have had as an infantryman. But that's the world we were in at that time, as these two guys end up as roommates at the St. George residence and become in charge of the social program. I graduated from law, Spring 1973. I then managed to land an articling job, a year at which was a prerequisite for bar admission.

» What happened in the summer of 1974? The resignation of Richard Nixon as president of the United States. Gerald Ford takes over. One of the first things he does is he pardons Nixon for any federal offences he had committed or might have committed. Lots of people were very angry with that: this head crook is getting off scot-free. His own underlings are being tried and sentenced. None of them was heavily sentenced in comparison to what they did, but he gets off scot-free. Less than a month later, President Ford gives us, the Vietnam War draft dodgers and deserters, conditional amnesty. I had to look into it.

I never thought we'd get any sort of amnesty, absolute or conditional, after only five years. I looked into it with the Toronto Anti-Draft Programme, which was then in Toronto's Yonge and Eglinton area.

I learned that at a few US Army posts, including Fort Dix, New Jersey, they were just throwing Vietnam-era deserters out of the Army with undesirable discharges, no questions asked, no punishment or conditions. Of course, this wasn't publicized because you couldn't publicize it, since this was easier on the deserters than the new official conditional amnesty program was.

So, having now found all that out, I'm now in the then six-month teaching term of Ontario's bar admission course. I'm finished with my articling work. Now I'm a studying student again, still existing on Canada student loans, Ontario student awards, and my summer jobs. My parents threw me 500 dollars a couple of times. I was very grateful. They would've given me whatever I asked, but I wasn't going to ask for a lot.

I decided to go to Fort Dix to get thrown out of the US Army. I went to see the director of the bar admission course, and I said, "I'm going to have to be away for a couple of weeks. I'm told it will take me a couple of weeks to get myself processed out of the US Army."

"Oh, don't worry, Johnny. Whatever." We had an exam once every two weeks or so. "Even if you miss an exam, you can make it up. Go. Good luck. Get this cleared up."

So I went to Fort Dix, New Jersey, mid-December 1974, almost exactly five years after I had deserted.

At Fort Dix, instead of taking two weeks, it took two days, because they had the same approach that Canada Immigration had had: "We'll send you the final paperwork in the mail. Keep us advised of your [American] address. But this is all in the bag, as from right now. You'll be in the army a few more weeks technically, but you're on unpaid leave in the meantime." I gave them one of my friends' address. The whole thing took two days. I was in the clear.

I've been back to the States many times as a visitor since.

Dean at home in Peterborough, Ontario. (Photo courtesy of Dean.)

12 Dean

I WAS BORN IN 1981 and spent most of my life in Saratoga Springs in upstate New York. I grew up in a military family in a sense: my stepfather was a contractor for the navy. He helped design and build the nuclear reactors in submarines. I got used to the mindset without really knowing the why, because he didn't wear the uniform himself. He simply worked alongside people that did. So he would emulate that somehow in his speech or in his mannerisms, and I'd just pick up on it without really knowing where it came from.

I started thinking about enlistment about two years before I was supposed to graduate high school. I was watching my sister struggle to find a college that would take her. She was getting 3.7, 3.8 GPA [grade point average]. She's a very smart girl, very book smart, and she was struggling. I saw her come home from some of the interviews in tears. And here I am with a much lower GPA, not really trying, didn't really care that much. I was like, Okay, well, smart as she is, and she can't find somewhere, there's no way I'm getting into college. There's no way I'm getting into SUNY [State University of New York] or anything. I might as well just join the military.

I think it's the reason a lot of people don't go for college, because if I screwed it up, then it was on me. I couldn't, I wouldn't burden my family with it, and I wouldn't max out credit cards and be drunk all the time. Military just seemed to be the easiest way out without stressing the family out more than they already were with my sister's stuff.

I enlisted with delayed entry in 1998. For two years I was considered inactive, until I went to boot camp. Basically, you just do meetings with your recruiters, and you go to the field to play soldier. You get to act a little bit foolish and enjoy yourself.

You get to know the recruiters a little bit through delayed entry. You get to know the reasons they joined. You get to meet a bigger pool of people because it's not just your little area, it's regional. You get to meet other people your own age, you know, "What did you join for? What are you gonna be doing?" It's kind of cool that way 'cause you start forming an early camaraderie with these people and start getting a sense of, okay, well, they're pretty much here for the same reason I am, so I must be on at least somewhat the right track. And you draw some comfort from that.

When I got to boot camp, I was 18. It was the 23rd of August. Three days later in boot camp, I turned 19. I ran the initial strength test on my birthday. I always thought that was funny, in an odd little way, to have a birthday. But you learn very quickly in boot camp, you don't tell them stuff like that. You don't say, "Hey, sir, it's my birthday," because you just know they're gonna mess with you that whole day or week. So I just kept my mouth shut about it.

Before I went to boot camp, I read this book called *Making the Corps*. I don't know if the recruiter gave me that book or if it was a family member. Maybe I just found it myself. I was a bookworm in those days, so it's possible I just found it in the library.

Because of that book, I felt like I had a pretty good idea of what to expect. And it was very accurate. Everything that was described in that book, in one way or another, did end up happening while I was there. I mean, it was still shocking; of course it is. Although a lot of the ways that they spoke, and a lot of the things they expected, I kind of already somewhat expected. Of course, not the yelling. You never get used to that, but just the regular day-to-day stuff, I kind of understood where they're coming from and where it was leading to. So because of that, it wasn't as big of a mystery as maybe it was for everybody else.

Boot camp in general was shocking. It's designed to shock you out of complacency, to shock you out of the usual. It quickly does that from day one. I'd like to think, you know, you're kind of on an even keel in life, and everything's either good or bad, and you're just kind of coasting along. But from the moment you get there, these big burly guys are screaming and yelling at you and throwing your stuff around. You come very quickly to "Okay, well, I have to pay attention now." No matter what, no matter how small a detail something is, no matter how insignificant it seems, there is no "insignificant" anymore. Everything's important. Everything's life or death. And from that point, everything is just like that. You just keep that mindset through the whole three months that you're dealing with it.

I think it's a shocking thing. You go from having a life where everything you do is more or less up to you, to now nothing is up to you. Not even down to what you call yourself. It's all dictated by somebody else that is a higher rank than you'll ever achieve. It's mind-bending, especially in the first few weeks. It's designed to break you down in the beginning and bring you into the ranks of something larger than yourself. As time goes on, there's the loss of individuality. They think it's key to building that team spirit for everything.

When you get there, you have no rank. The reason they do that is because, of course, if you had rank, you would be considered "in." And if you were in, they wouldn't be allowed to do the things that they do. Basically, they're allowed to haze you because you're not in. They can do whatever they want to you, and there's really no repercussions for them if they go too far. You know, step over the line, and supposedly it builds a team spirit. I don't know how accurate that is.

I joined the Marine Corps to work on computers. Initially, they stuck me with telephones and switchboards. Later on, after boot camp, after all the schooling, the first posting was to Japan, to Okinawa, in 2001. It was at that point that they merged telephones and computers together. So in a roundabout way, I got what I wanted. I spent a year there from August 2001 to August 2002. After that it was Camp Lejeune in North Carolina. I was stationed there until 2006. But from there, you deploy to other places. I deployed for the ground war in Iraq in 2003, then to Landstuhl Regional Medical Center in 2004, and then Iraq again in 2005. Again, all from Lejeune, the main base. You get sent wherever the heck they feel like sending you. Once Lejeune was finished, they sent me to a reserve station farther inland in North Carolina to help train reservists in the repair of computers, telephones, that sort of thing.

Every Marine served in Okinawa for one year, whether you want to or not. Iraq, for the ground war, was six months. I remember being pretty surprised by that. I always thought that war would be a long, drawn-out thing, but it really wasn't that way.

Germany was only a few months. I was having trouble adjusting, so they kind of took pity on me and sent me back stateside. The final Iraq tour was just over a year.

It was weird, because in Okinawa, in 2001, I was in the barracks, I was on the phone with my parents, and somebody came running in and said these words: "Somebody has bombed the World Trade Center again," referring back to the bombing in '93. I thought, Okay, well, that's kind of scary. My parents were in Connecticut at the time. They were safe, and they probably didn't know any more than I did. I ran upstairs to my room. I had just gotten the internet set up. The first tower was already smoking, and I'm sitting there watching it, thinking, How do they get a bomb halfway up a building? That's just silly. And then, on air, like, in front of me, the second plane hit the tower, and I was like, "Holy crap, a plane just ran into a building."

It was chaotic for the first few days because nobody knew where it came from, nobody knew what happened. All bases overseas immediately went on lockdown. We weren't allowed out in town anymore. We weren't allowed out of uniform anymore. Everybody was pulled from their jobs. I had been repairing computers, but all regular activity stopped. Everybody was pulled to do gate guard, fence patrol. It became about protecting the base, like they're coming for us next. In that moment, that's just the mindset America had: "Oh my God, everything is under attack right now, do something." It was just all patrols, guarding the compound.

On the night before we were scheduled to ship out—February, I think—George Bush got on TV and said that he wanted military—Marines, airmen—on the ground in Iraq, and he wanted them to have all the support staff they needed. He was the president. He was in charge of us. No formal issue orders had been written or sent. But just because that man went on TV and said that, he cancelled a whole ship movement. We were all sent back to our parent commands and basically told to wait by our phone: "We're gonna be calling you, you're going somewhere else, you're doing something else. We don't know where, but you're going somewhere."

I'm an electronic tech. As much as they like to say every Marine is a rifleman, it was very much an office job. I had a cubicle. I fix computers and stuff with a soldering iron. It wasn't a very dangerous job really. And that was kind of my foolish mistake, because you can be called upon to do anything. I didn't realize the scope of what that meant until the ground war. They said, "Instead of repairing computers and telephones, you're gonna be a military policeman running convoys." I asked them if they could just make me switch roles like that. Is that even a thing? "Oh yeah, we can make you do anything we want to. Now you're just gonna go protect convoys through Mosul and Baghdad and whatnot. What do you think of that?" I'm like, "Guess I don't really have much of a choice in the matter."

With very little training and very little support, they made me and a bunch of my friends military policemen, to run convoys from Kuwait into Iraq. That was in the early days, when we didn't know what was even in Iraq. It was just that sudden and that bizarre.

Back then we were told that there were weapons of mass destruction, and that Saddam Hussein had all sorts of chemical weapons, and of course he didn't. But at the time we had to pretend like there was. That was the fear. The early days were scarier. Once the Iraq army was defeated, it really wasn't as big of a concern that you might have missiles lobbed at you. It was then just occasional potshots from the side of the road.

There's always surprises in the military.

After my first tour in Iraq, I went back for about a year. The next deployment was Germany. I was getting ready to get out of the Marines, but they offered me a huge amount of money to stay put. I was doing pretty well at the time. I think I had just picked up Corporal. Everything was going as well as could be expected, and then a friend of mine came around and said, "Hey, what do you think about going to Germany?" I was like, "Well, seems a little weird, we don't normally go to Germany as Marines, but okay."

He had mentioned that we'd be working in the hospitals. I said, "That's even weirder, because we don't have medical staff. That's not even our thing." But it turned out they just wanted liaisons between the injured coming in and the hospital staff, somebody that spoke the language between the doctors and the wounded. I thought, Okay, well, how bad can it be? We're gonna go help people, which is awesome. That's what you want to do with your life: you wanna be able to help people. So it was that abrupt: we're going to Germany in two weeks, in 2004.

My original contract was supposed to end in 2005. My friend said, "Your enlistment's up next year, so in order to qualify for that, they'd need you to re-enlist." When you go through the process, you have to meet with a career planner. He said, "Well, you're a comm guy. So there's a $15,000 bonus if you're re-enlisted." I'd never seen $15,000 before in my life. And you're telling me if I just stay here and do what I was going to do anyway? Okay. Fifteen grand is fifteen grand! So because of the money, and because of the fact that I was going to go to Germany, I ended up signing a new contract, which took my remaining time and added four more years. So that put the contract up in 2009.

I was never really trained in medical stuff. I mean, you're trained as a field medic for basic stuff. But I don't think there's anything that really prepares you for that sort of work. I thought, Hey, at least you're not getting shot at or shooting anybody. I'll play along, and I'll go do it.

It was me, my sergeant, and a staff sergeant that worked out of Bethesda Medical. I was only there for a few months. At first it was what I expected: there are people that come in wounded, missing arms or legs, and their first question is, "Okay what do I do now?" We direct them: "Welcome to Germany, here's your first appointment, tomorrow at 6:00. I'm going to be driving you to that. Here's a phone card, you can call your family, we've already paid for your mother's flight here. She's coming in, and she's going to see you tomorrow morning." We basically made sure everything that they could be worried about was dealt with. We even followed up: "Well, here's the time you take your medication, here's the times we're coming to check on you." These people were scared, and they think they're going to die. If they wanted a pencil eraser, I'd go get it, if it made one minute of happiness for them. That's the job. It was very humanizing in a not very human occupation: something good.

It is very emotional, but rewarding in its own way. You're actually helping people. There was an amazing feeling that I've never actually felt. You know, it's not soul enriching by any means when you fix somebody's telephone, but then there's a scared 19-year-old kid missing a foot. He's terrified. Some of them actually thought they were in trouble for getting shot. It's like, "No man, you're not in trouble. Stuff happens. You're wounded. We're gonna take care of you. Your meeting with your prosthetic guy is at 6:00 tomorrow. No problem. Don't sweat it." And just seeing the look of "Okay, I'm not in trouble, everything's going to be fine. My parents are coming." It's an amazing feeling, seeing them come down from being in a combat zone to being like, "Okay, well, everything's fine, everything's taken care of." It's emotionally draining, but also very emotionally rewarding.

Jobs like that, they do take a lot out of you, and as time progressed, some of the casualties got worse. Some of the casualties started becoming children. That's kind of when things went off the rails for me.

About a month into me being there, there was a bombing at a tent city somewhere outside of Mosul. There were strong prevailing winds that day, and for whatever reason their waterproof of choice for their tents is kerosene. So all these tents went up. Then you started seeing the adults come in, young adults and teenagers, and then eventually you get to a point where there's literally busloads coming in from this—all burnt, bloody. You can't tell that they're human beings, some of them. I saw two guys with a stretcher carrying this black thing. It looked like a trash bag to me, and it turns out it's an infant, burned to hell. You can't identify it, but it's alive. You know it's alive because it's screaming. That changes your attitude towards the government in a big damn hurry. At least it did for me.

You hear the phrase "collateral damage," and you just assume somebody's building got knocked over. That sucks! Or someone's house got blown up. I'm sure we'll pay them. I'm sure we'll help them move or something. Then you realize collateral damage also means people: people that weren't in the military, who had nothing to do with it and were just trying to live out their life the same way I was. Their reward for staying out of it is, here's a bomb in your living room. You can't justify it at that point. I couldn't. There's nothing that country ever did wrong to me that justifies anything. It's like if somebody let off a bomb in Buffalo. What's Buffalo ever done to me? What's Buffalo ever done to you? It's not right. No matter the reasoning, it's not right.

I think it was a pretty violent shift for me. I mean, up until then you kind of have your doubts over time because, as you watch the news, well, no weapons were found. Okay, we're on the wrong side of morality here.

Because of those incidents, a straight week of that nonsense, I zoned out at work. I wasn't really paying attention. I wasn't visiting the patients like I was supposed to. Eventually, the master sergeant in charge took me aside and said, "I don't think you're doing too well with this stuff." I wasn't. I think this is messing me up somehow, and I don't know how. I'm not sleeping, I'm not eating. Nothing seems to matter. In a real human moment, in a realm pretty much devoid of it, he said, "You know, we're gonna send you back stateside so you can maybe talk to somebody, get some help. Because that was a pretty messed-up week." So I got sent back. It was only two months later. I couldn't even stay for the full time.

I didn't know how to deal with it. I didn't even know how to ask other people how to deal with it. Because, again, we're not very medically minded folks. So I didn't know. I was torn between wanting to tell somebody about this stuff and worrying that they're gonna think I'm crazy, and they're gonna kick me out, and I'll never be able to get a pension. You worry that it's just you, you're just the crazy person and that's all there is to it. Just "Oh, just, you know, go get some sleep. You know, drink some water and everything will be fine." It just never actually did go away, which is what I was hoping. I did ask once if I could maybe see somebody. But nothing ever came of it. It took a long time to realize that it's not something that goes away. At the time I didn't even know what it was, I didn't know there's a name for it. That's just how ignorant I was of everything.

I didn't find out until two years later that it'd end up being post-traumatic stress. I assumed that was something that happened only to people that opened fire or took fire. It took me years to find that out.

I got put on a roster when I came back to Lejeune. I got back in January 2005 and had to leave in August the same year. I found during those eight months there was actually more training, not so much on the combat stuff, but about the history of Iraq: these are the people, these are the local laws. The first time we went over, we didn't know anything about anything, and it led to a lot of misunderstandings, and a lot of trouble that shouldn't have happened. And so, the second time around,

I was actually kind of relieved that there was some cultural education to prepare ourselves a little bit for the Iraqis we'd see on base. It definitely felt safer. But, I mean, it's still Iraq, and you still don't want to let people know that you're crazy. At the time I considered myself to be crazy because I didn't know another word for it.

That year in Iraq was just no fun for me. I'm sure the command probably noticed it, but there wasn't anything he could've done. We were already deployed. My mental health that year was very tenuous. I felt I finally got it into my head that I should talk to the priest. At the time that just seemed like the most reasonable thing. I found the navy chaplain of the base on Al-Asad at the time and spoke to him. He said, "Oh, you just sound like you're trying to go home." I really wasn't. I wasn't trying to go home, and I didn't feel suicidal. But that's very much the attitude they take: "Oh, you're just trying to get out of something. You're supposed to go to a combat zone tomorrow. It sounds like you're trying to get out." I wasn't trying to get out of anything. I just wanted help. He's like, "Well, you know, just get out of my office. You're a coward, I don't want to talk to you!"

So there was a lot of internalizing. I had a night shift for a lot of the time I was there. I had a lot of time to myself, and I was just staring at the walls and reliving everything. It's just no good for anybody. There were a couple of times I remember staring at the wall when I first got there, and then somehow, 12 hours later, somebody came up and was like, "Hey, time to go home." Twelve hours already? They were spent lost in my own thoughts, having accomplished nothing that night. I didn't hang out with anybody from my unit. I stayed separate from them as much as I could. The moment that we got released from work, I'd go to one of the park benches or something. I did anything to get away from people so I didn't have to feel so crowded, so personally invaded. I just wanted to be left alone. I was trying to find quiet, and there is no such place on a military base.

When I got back to Lejeune, I got orders to change units, to change commands, not deploy, but to go to a new base. Oddly enough, it was Okinawa. They wanted me to go back to Japan. I wrote to the powers that be and explained that I'd been deployed four times in my five years, and that I just wanted to stay stateside. He wrote back: "I've got this great reserve unit that's about four hours from where you are now. You'll never have to deploy there as an active-duty person. You're just helping the reservists there that might deploy, refreshing their skills in repair." I was like, "Okay, well, that sounds pretty calm." It wasn't a base; it was 12 people in an office, almost like a recruiting station. If I couldn't find peace and quiet in a college town like Greensboro, something's really wrong. So I accepted the orders.

There, it became very easy to see it as a 9 to 5 job, where at five o'clock you're not a Marine anymore, you're just a civilian living in a college town. And because of that it was very easy to find some measure of peace. There wasn't even a barracks. We had to actually live out in town in an apartment that we got to choose ourselves. I'd never had that much freedom in the Marine Corps. I actually made some friends within the command itself. I was actually kind of friendly to these people that, traditionally, I wouldn't have dared talk to on Lejeune because they were too high up.

I told them about these weird dreams I was getting some days. They were actually okay with what I was telling them. The first question from all of them was "Are you suicidal? If you're suicidal, there's stuff we have to do." I was legitimately not suicidal, and I don't feel I ever was. I just wanted help. I wanted to know what this was. I wanted to know how to make it go away. That's how naive I was. Eventually, they sent me to a civilian psychiatrist, who diagnosed it as PTSD, and anti-social behaviour due to PTSD, where I was trying to stay away from people. I was put on Zoloft. They signed me up for biweekly counselling meetings.

But over time, the command stopped letting me go to [the psychiatrist], because it was during work hours. They wanted me to do it outside of work hours, but their work hours and the psychiatrist's were the same. He was about 20 minutes away, so there's just no way. By that point, I think the command had simply got tired of me talking about it: "You got your medicine, shut up." It became very icy there over a very short period of time.

I became isolated. I lived by myself, and the only roommate I had was a rabbit. I don't know what possessed me to buy the rabbit. I guess that was my idea of outreach. Something to talk to when I got home. At first, once I had the diagnosis, I assumed, "Okay, well, you know you're still nuts, but at least you know what it is now. They're not letting you go to counselling, of course, but you're on this medicine. Eventually, over time, it'll just go away, and everything will be peachy keen. I just gotta be patient and let these things run their course."

That's when mortuary affairs decided to enter my life one more time.

There was a phone call that came down saying that we had to take four reservists and activate them to full duty. And their job wasn't gonna be electronic. It was going to be going after the Humvees that were blown up from the IEDs [improvised explosive devices] to remove the bodies. I'm like, "Mortuary affairs, are you kidding me? This crap again." Here I am, I think I'm crazy, I'm medicated, but, you know, mortuary affairs is following me again. Although I'm safe because I'm in a reserve unit, but now we're sending these 18-, 19-year-old reservists. I know a lot of them from town: a lot of full families, kids and wife and the whole thing. It's bad enough if *I* die. I'm just a single guy at the time, who cares. Nobody's devastated. But it's fathers, sons. So here I am, nice and safe and sound, and here's these ill-trained reservists being sent to do this crap, and it's just reminding me of all the stuff they sent me to do—craziness that I had no business doing. I realized how much that was probably messing them up. And I think it was about that time where it just became enough. I just got fed up with the whole thing.

I don't think I had any clear idea of what I was going to do at the time. I was researching, hoping to find some weird loophole or something just to get out. Of course, no such loophole existed, but it doesn't stop you from googling when you live on your own with a rabbit. So I spent a lot of time googling ways to get out legally, and conscientious objection came up. But nobody takes that seriously. The longest-running joke in the military is C.O. status. You can't apply for that; you can't even do that. You can't even ask for those forms, because the minute you do, you flag yourself as being the platoon asshole, and nothing you want from that point on is gonna matter. Your career is over at that point. So there's no point even asking for it. And even if you did ask for it, at least for the Marines, the first step is to be placed in a non-combative unit. I already did that, and I still want out. The next step is to kick you out, and they're not gonna do that after all that training and all that money.

I distinctly remember showing up to work and being constantly angry and saying these words: "One of these days, you guys are coming to work, and I'm gonna be in Canada. And on that day, I don't want you complaining."

Before talking to anyone from the [War Resisters Support] Campaign, I did notice a thing in the American mindset: people went to Vietnam, and they went to Canada to get out of Vietnam, and I knew a little bit about it. Then I said it'd be funny if I'd just go to Canada. I'm done with this stuff. I hadn't really made any sort of plans to actually come to Canada. I didn't realize it was even an option. I assumed I'd get arrested at the border, so I didn't give it much thought until I started just randomly googling words like "trying to find a way to get out" or "desert." I spent months at the computer, just trying to find some way to get out. Also, GI Rights [Network]—of course there's that [hotline] phone number, but they're not very helpful either. I was facing a lot of despair, a lot of soul searching: Do you want to do this anymore? Shouldn't we be done with this crap by now? I felt a lot of bitterness towards the whole command because here I am: I'm crazy and not getting help. It was a confluence of so many things at once.

Through googling I found a website called resisters.ca. At first I was kind of paranoid. I thought maybe it was some sort of a military police trap to catch deserting people. But I found a number of an office that was in Toronto. I debated it for a few days and decided, What the hell? I gave them a call.

I think the very first person I ever talked to at the War Resisters Support Campaign was Lee. He explained his own reasons for coming to Canada. It sort of mirrored the current situation. It was kind of nice, because there was a first moment of actual legitimate "Okay, well, I'm not so crazy. At least I'm not as crazy as I thought I was because some of the things I feel are some of the things others feel." Then he introduces me over the phone to other US war resisters. I would not be here today if not for them. They gave me a lot of information. They had me read up on some of the history of resisting the Vietnam War. I felt in a weird way I found a home. I found a home over the phone with a group of people that I recognized as being like-minded.

Those conversations went on until December 1 or 2, 2006. It was a Friday. I talked to Michelle that day and she asked, "Do you think you're going to do it? You think you're gonna come up here? Because we need to plan things out a bit." It's like, I honestly don't know. I didn't know what I was gonna do. She said, "Okay, well, why don't you spend the next few days thinking about it and, you know, give us a call, let us know what you think, and we can go from there. Just know whatever you decide, we're gonna be there for you."

I took the weekend to think about it. I thought about it right up 'til Monday morning. I was supposed to go to work Monday morning. I was wearing the shirt and the shorts because we're supposed to go for a run as a unit that day around town. The night before, I was watching the movie *Office Space*. The next morning, as I'm getting ready to eat before we went on this run, I was staring at the toaster, waiting for it to pop up. I remember thinking back to the scene where they're in the restaurant, towards the beginning of the movie, and she's like, "What do you do for your job?" And he's explaining that he helped to write Year 2000 code. Then he breaks from that and says, "You know what, I don't like talking about my job. I don't like my job at all. I don't think I'm going to go back. I don't think I'm going to go to work." And she just kind of laughs about that. She asks, "Aren't you gonna get fired?" He's like, "I don't know. I know I don't want to go." And she says something to the effect of "What about your bills?" "I don't like paying bills either! I don't think I'm going to do that anymore either." You know, it's not a movie to be taken seriously at all, but somehow in that moment it's like, "God, I identify with that. I don't want to go. I don't want to go to work. I don't want to. I don't want this anymore. I don't want this life. I think I'm done. I don't know what's going to happen, but I know right now in this moment I'm done." And that was enough. Somehow, that goofy-ass movie was enough to just push everything over the edge.

You know, let the chips fall where they may. I've had enough of this. I'd rather be in jail. If they come for me, they come for me. I'm done. So I'm sitting there in skivvy shorts, trying to cram everything quickly into a bag so I can make the bus. I call Michelle: "I'm coming right now." From the time I had my aha moment to me actually getting on a Greyhound [bus] and leaving was about 14 hours.

I left just about everything in the apartment. I left the rabbit with a friend that later on became my best man at my wedding. I left it with him.

I didn't tell him what was going on. I didn't want to. I didn't want anyone to know.

Even having been in a combat zone, it's the only time in my life I've been truly terrified. It became a big thing in my mind that they're going to find me. I'd made these bizarre plans in my head that I was gonna walk through the woods to get to the Greyhound station. I was just paranoid. I knew, first off, I couldn't be at the apartment because that would be the first place they'd look. I also knew I couldn't tell my parents. If I told my parents, then they'd feel obligated to tell the command. I spent the whole next 14 hours paranoid because the first bus going to Canada was at 4 p.m. I had made this decision at, like, 6:00 in the morning. I'd actually just changed banks the day before, so I didn't even have a bank card to get the money out to pay for the Greyhound. So the first couple of hours were spent shivering outside of the bank, waiting for it to open so I could get the money out of the bank. I didn't want to go in, because then the camera would see me, and they'd report me to the police. Eventually, I just got so cold that I decided I had to risk it, and I went inside a hotel lobby, where they probably thought I was homeless, because they offered me food. They told me to go get the free continental breakfast. They must have thought I was a hobo—that's the only thing that ever made sense to me. So I just sat inside there, eating free breakfast food, until the bank opened.

I had one little bag with me. I had a very military haircut at the time. I was trying not to make things too obvious, so I figured a small bag would probably erase suspicion. I was terrified that somebody was gonna rat me out.

The bank finally opened. Then I got the money out. The guy asked me why I was taking all the money out if I just opened the account. "Oh, I'm going on vacation." "Where's the vacation?" "Canada." "It's December." "Yeah." "Okay, enjoy your vacation, I guess." It's a weird place to go in December...I didn't know what else to tell the guy.

Then I went to the bus station. I guess it was about 11-ish by that time. The lady behind the counter ended up coming up to me after about 30 minutes, telling me that some of the other passengers in the bus terminal were complaining because I was acting paranoid. Any time the door would slam or would open, I'd apparently act strange. So they literally kicked me out of the Greyhound bus terminal because I was freaking people out. I was scaring people without realizing it.

So I went to a bar that was down the road. I just sat down next to this guy and started drinking. We talked about whatever game was on TV. I don't remember. And I guess by that point I was pretty well lit because I looked at the guy. I had my hat off, I had a bag next to me. I asked, "What do you do when you can't take your job anymore?" And he looked at me. He's like, "You just gotta walk away, man. If it's that bad. Don't do it. It's not worth your health. It's not worth your life." That's the first calming, sensical thing I'd heard all day. That was it. That was the real moment it was done in my mind. That's when all the fear vanished and it became real obvious: Yeah, you're getting on this bus today.

I got on the bus. I paid with cash, of course, because I was terrified that they would trace the account. I got my 15 percent military discount for the last time. I got on the bus on a 28-hour bus ride up here.

I crossed the border from Detroit into Windsor, Ontario. I remember in the back of my head I had a conversation earlier with Michelle on the phone, talking about, "When you get off the bus they're going to ask you what you're here for. You tell them you're just gonna come see a friend. If they ask you if you're staying, you say no. If they ask you what you've brought, don't argue, just let them look in your bag. Be polite but don't give away anything."

I'm kind of nervous at this point, because this seems like the real moment where getting into trouble is actually possible. So I get off the bus. I had my military ID and my licence in my hand, getting ready to explain myself.

We're all in this big lineup to this counter, and there's this woman in front of me. She hands her ID over. I've never gotten a clear sense of this, but apparently there's some device or something that they use that lets you know if you have drugs on your person or if you used your ID to cut drugs. This woman popped positive for some reason or another. She starts freaking out in this customs terminal, then six or seven burly guys come and drag her away. She's kicking and screaming, hair is flying everywhere, bags are all over the damn place. And I'm just scared pantless at this point, 'cause I'm next. They finally drag her off.

The guy at the counter? His shirt's all dishevelled, his tie is ripped to hell. He just looks like crap. He's like, "So how are you doing? Coming to visit Canada?" "Yeah, I'm coming." He's like, "What do you have in the bag?" "Oh, just some clothes and a book." "Welcome to Canada, please get the hell back on the bus." I think at that point the guy had just had enough of that particular bus. So the border crossing itself, after all the worrying I did, was not as big of a deal as it could have been.

» Going AWOL was my first time in Canada. Even though I lived in upstate New York, nobody ever said, "Let's go visit Canada. Let's go to Quebec. Let's go get drunk in Ontario." That never happened. Nobody ever said that. I wouldn't have known how to get there anyway.

Eventually, I ended up in Toronto. I met Michelle there. She was waiting at the bottom of the bus stairs. I think she was afraid I'd get lost or something. I met her, hugged her, and said thank you. The very first day I was in Canada, there was already a meeting going on, a Resisters meeting. I didn't even have a health card yet, but I'm already in counselling of a sort. That was a big drastic change going from "Shut up, shut up, shut up," to "Hey, welcome to this meeting, here's some coffee or some cookies, tell us about yourself." It's mind-bending that anybody would actually care enough about me to ask those kinds of questions.

I didn't really know the place very well. I had to get used to the idea of a subway system. I've only visited New York City a few times and never had to use the subway at all. So that was a new experience. The Resisters put me in touch with a couple of professors from the University of Toronto who had an extra room in their basement. They very graciously let me stay there for a couple of weeks until I got a little more established. I didn't start working right away, just because I had just gotten there, and all the offices for immigration were pretty much closed for the holidays. So I couldn't even start the immigration process really. I was just a guy in Canada. I couldn't do much of anything but just wait. So for a lot of the time I just bummed around the city, finding out where the stores around me were and basically waiting for the next War Resisters meeting. I think being deployed to other countries kind of helped a little. Because after you deploy to so many countries that are so different, you come to Canada and the language is the same. The money is slightly different, but there's a lot of commonalities really. So it made the transition not as bad as it could have been.

After a week or two, I finally contacted my family. I didn't want to get them in trouble. By the time I called my mom, she informed me that the command had already called them, wanting to know if I was there. Of course they told the truth: they had no idea where I was. They assumed I was deployed somewhere. I didn't tell them, I didn't tell my sister. I guess that was pretty hard for them at first. They understood it though. They were supportive. I was kind of surprised by that—again, coming from a quasi-military family. I thought I'd get more flak than that, especially from my stepdad. He actually understood the decision.

I had to wait for the holidays to be over before the immigration offices finally opened. My lawyer at the time gave me this big stack of paperwork to bring to immigration at the airport. I remember spending a lot of time at the airport. I hated that bus ride. I didn't have the support necessary to do the paperwork. It was just me guessing a lot of it. The Campaign certainly helped where they could. I guess the first time I went to immigration I was probably scared. I assumed they were just gonna tell me "No" right then and there, not having a lawyer with me or anything. But they couldn't have been nicer about it. They didn't give me that much fuss.

In 2007, I filed a refugee claim. It has to be approved by them. For the first several years here, five, maybe even six years, I was a refugee claimant. Whether or not they approve it is another matter.

Where my case ended up going through the refugee claim is a bit of a mystery even to me. I know that it went pretty high up in the courts. I received a letter saying, "Here's the date that you have to get out of our country by. We expect you to report at the Niagara Falls office: we expect you to leave at this point." That was terrifying: "Oh my God, they're kicking me out." By that point I had switched lawyers over to Alyssa Manning. She's awesome. I switched over to her and she started the appeals process. Next thing you know, after two straight weeks of being scared, they said, "You don't have to leave now. You start the process over." That would happen three times throughout the ten years I've been in the system. Three separate times where they've told me to leave and then been like, "Never mind." And I think by the third time you just kind of get tired of it. So after a while, you just kind of put it out of your head and focus on your day. You can't live in fear like that all the time. It's not good for you.

I've been in Canada for a little over 11 years—11 years and a week [at time of recording], and I don't regret it. Honestly, I love it here. I wouldn't want to live anywhere else. It's a very laid-back country, and everybody has been very accepting. I have no regrets about any of it.

Canada feels like another deployment, a longer-term deployment. I don't know again if it feels like there's a sense of home here. In talking with the Campaign and the friends of the Campaign, it's a great big family. It comes out of a morality-based world view, and I love the idea of that. You're not hurting me, I'm not hurting you, everything's fine. And it just befuddles me that it ever seemed so complicated before. Being an American, everybody hates you and there's no reason why. And then you think, well, there are some valid reasons. But we [Canadians] don't care where you're from. We're just happy you're here and not causing trouble. That's like a big Canadian thing: just don't cause trouble. We don't care what you do, just don't make anybody's life difficult. That's an amazing thing to walk into after being American and having everything so strict, and having your world view be very pro-American: we're great, we're awesome, and it's crap.

In the time I've had here, I've had a chance to do some healing. I felt pretty isolated being in the military in the States and having PTSD in general. But whereas that culture is very much a macho culture of "Shut up, we don't want to hear about it, just do your job," coming here to Canada, it's been very different. Not only are you *not* told to be quiet; thanks to the Campaign you end up doing speaking events at universities and colleges and a lot of radio and TV interviews. So the need for therapy over time sort of diminished, because everybody wanted to talk about it. You get a telephone, you get to tell these stories, maybe you laugh a little bit, maybe you cry a little bit. It certainly was a lot of crying the first couple of interviews I did, but I'm not ashamed to admit that. It becomes so helpful to be surrounded by this incredible amount of support.

I don't really consider myself American anymore either. I think I kind of left that behind. I can't really consider myself American anymore. I don't consider myself Canadian. I don't really look at it that way. And I can't really, in good conscience, call myself Canadian either, because I'm not fully Canadian yet. I haven't gone through that process just yet. But I've come to realize that that distinction is not really meaningful in any way. I mean, I can't wait to be legally Canadian, but I'm more or less content now calling myself Canadian, not American. I don't know if you need to necessarily identify with a particular culture or a particular country. I'm just happy that this country has decided to step in and accept me. I hope I become more Canadian as time goes on.

I definitely plan on applying for my Canadian citizenship. I'm in college now, and I'm hoping, for one of the electives, I get to take Canadian history, because apparently that's a big part of the citizenship test. Sadly, I know very little about it. Because in America you're not taught other countries' histories. You just hold your own, so you don't know anything about the world at large. I think that is at least part of the problem and part of what drove me up here: that level of ignorance. Now that I'm here, I'm hoping to shed that ignorance.

I do have a Canadian-born wife, daughter, and two boys. They're all healthy and happy. The little ones don't understand everything that has happened in the first eight or nine years of their life. They don't understand, and I don't plan on explaining that to them until they're older. For now, to them, I'm Dad. I'm not a veteran to them, I'm not American to them, I'm not even really Canadian to them. I'm just Dad.

Joe at work as a judge at the courthouse the year before he retired.
(Photo by Alison Mountz.)

13 Joe

YOU RARELY MEET PEOPLE that are still thinking about the war in Vietnam these days.

I was born in 1947 in Pensacola, Florida. My mother was from El Salvador, my dad was American. When I was three months old, we moved to El Salvador. Until age 11, I stayed mainly in El Salvador. Then my father got a job in Los Angeles, so we all moved, and I stayed there until I went into the army in 1967.

I was very happy in Los Angeles, but then the Vietnam War started to increase in intensity. After I graduated from high school, I went to Los Angeles City College, so I had a student deferment. And then halfway through my education at Los Angeles City College, I decided that I would apply to become a Jesuit priest. I was so confident that I was going to be accepted that I quit school. I went to Alabama to visit my parents and wait for what I thought was going to be my acceptance by the Jesuits.

They didn't accept me. And there I was, with no deferment. So I was going to be drafted, and I had developed a strong moral difficulty with the war. But I didn't want to go to jail or leave the country because I was very happy in Los Angeles. All my friends were there. So I tried to figure out a way that I could have my cake and eat it too. I decided that maybe if I agreed to go into the army and become a medic, then it would be okay, morally speaking. I knew that if you enlisted, they would give you your choice of jobs in the army. If you were drafted, they wouldn't give you your choice. You would most probably be in the infantry.

So I enlisted. They guaranteed that I could become a medic. I took all the tests and they said that I could basically choose any job in the army. But in keeping with my plan, I decided to be a combat medic. I went into basic training at Fort Ord, and then I went to AIT [advanced infantry training] at Fort Sam Houston. Then they sent me to Vietnam in December of 1968.

I arrived in Vietnam, and I was assigned to a platoon in the jungle about 23 miles southwest of Saigon, as it was then called.

I started going out on line. After a few firefights and seeing the devastation that was occurring, not only to our troops but to the enemy's troops and also to the villagers, I couldn't help but conclude that what I was doing was wrong, even though I was a medic and I wasn't carrying any kind of firearm. Even though I wasn't actually shooting at people, I was part of the team, and I felt morally wrong.

When I was in Vietnam, a lot of people asked me why I didn't carry a rifle or not even a .45 that they issued to the medics. I didn't carry one primarily because I wasn't going to use it, because I was against killing people. The second reason I didn't carry is because, as a medic, I was so busy tending to the people that were injured that I didn't have time to be shooting at anybody. I depended on the other members of my squad and my platoon to protect me. And they did protect you, because you were the one that was gonna help them to stay alive if they got injured. The medics also have their medics bag. And it was just too much junk to be carrying around with you.

Once, we were pinned down in a firefight. I was on the ground next to my second lieutenant. He asked me why I didn't carry a gun. I told him that I didn't want to kill people, just save lives. He told me that just because I didn't carry a gun didn't mean that I was better than the rest of the guys with respect to killing people. I was part of the team. That really started me thinking, and I realized he was right. I was part of the team. My job was just a different one. And I think that was the beginning of the end of my participation in the war. It really hit me hard. I realized that I was a hypocrite. That really spurred me on to my decision not to go back out on line anymore.

I was still a practising Catholic when I was in Vietnam. They had priests who would come out and say mass for us. And one day a priest was saying mass. And at the moment of the elevation, where he holds up the host, I heard machine-gun fire going on. And in that moment it just crystallized in my mind that the Catholic Church was complicit as much as I was, being a medic. I saw a bit of a parallel there. Here we had Catholic priests saying mass, supposedly teaching Christ's teachings, who was completely non-violent. And I realized that there was something seriously wrong with my spiritual leaders. Before that moment, the fact that they were present was comforting. But at that moment, I realized that it was absurd to feel comforted by a priest who was supposed to be a representative of Christ and to be encouraged by their presence to continue fighting and helping to kill people.

Those two things really marked me. They were very important moments for me in making the decision that I made not to go back out on line.

So I decided to refuse to go out on the line. I told my superiors that I was not going to go on line anymore. They reacted in various ways. Some of them just thought I was afraid. Some took a gentler approach and tried to counsel me and gave me some time to think about it. But I just refused steadfastly to participate anymore. After about a week of refusal, they sent me to the rear in Củ Chi.

I stayed there, and they continued to try to give me appointments with counsellors and psychologists. They sent me to talk to a priest. All of this was geared towards trying to help me to rearrange my thoughts and go back out on line. But I kept telling them that I wasn't interested in talking to counsellors and priests. I'd made up my mind. I wasn't afraid. I wasn't crazy. I wasn't having an emotional breakdown. I had just made a moral decision. After that they started offering me alternative jobs. They told me, "Okay, you don't have to go back on line. You can go work in a hospital in the rear. You can become part of an artillery unit." I guess they thought that basically I was afraid to go on line, and that was the reason motivating my decision. But I told them that I felt that that would still be contributing to the war effort and therefore morally wrong, and I couldn't do it.

So they told me, "Well, the only thing left is that we're going to give you a direct order to go back on line. If you refuse, stockade." So I said, "Fine. Give me the direct order, and we'll see what happens from there." The day before they told me that they were going to order me to go back on line, I was in the barracks talking to the doctor that was the captain of my medical platoon. I was kind of joking around with him actually, and I said, "It's too bad that I'm not going on leave or for R and R." He was sympathetic to me; he was against the war as well. And he said, "You've just given me an idea. I'm going to talk to somebody that I know." He came back and told me that a colonel he knew wanted to see me and wanted me to explain to him what I was thinking and what my problem was.

I went to see the colonel, and I told the colonel the same thing I'd been telling everybody else: that I was morally against the war. I wasn't going to take an easy job in the rear. That wasn't the point. He thought about it and he said, "Well, I will grant you a leave, a seven-day leave. What are you going to do with it?" And I said, "Well, you know, I'm going to go to Hawaii. I'll ask my parents to come to Hawaii. And we'll talk, get my head straight, and then come back." I lied. I'm pretty sure he knew I was lying. And he said, "All right, I'll grant you leave, you go to meet your parents, get your head straight, and come back."

Right after I talked to the colonel about my leave to Hawaii, I left his office, and outside "Blowin' in the Wind" by Bob Dylan was playing on the radio of one of the soldiers. That was an important moment for me. I thought that that was a good omen.

I did not have the cash to buy a ticket to Hawaii. My friend, a fellow medic, gave me $500 to buy a ticket from Saigon to Honolulu. Decades later, my wife surprised me with a reunion in Toronto with this friend, and with the doctor of my medical platoon, so that I could thank him all those years later.

I went to Hawaii. I didn't meet my parents there. That was never part of my plan.

I stayed in Hawaii for a while, trying to make myself look like a civilian. After about six days, though, I called my parents and told them where I was and that I wanted to come see them.

They wired me some money somehow. I went to see them, and it wasn't until I got to their house in Alabama that I told them what I had done. They were always anti-war, so they were very happy that I had deserted. They never wanted me to go in the first place.

I stayed with them for a few days. I knew that in 14 days the army would send somebody to your home to look for you, because that's where they caught most of the guys that went AWOL. I told my parents that I had to get out of there soon, or else they were going to come get me and catch me there. So I rented a little motel unit in a nearby town so I could stay just a little longer and try to figure out what I was going to do next. After much talking, we decided that the best place for me to go would be to Canada. My father heard that the Canadian government was sympathetic to draft dodgers and deserters, and that the chances were pretty good that I'd be able to settle there.

I was driving around in my dad's Volkswagen and decided to go to the beach one day just to think about things. I parked in the parking lot and just sat there looking at the ocean and everything. Then I see in the rearview mirror a police car pulling up behind me. The lights start going and everything. The policeman comes over and asks what I'm doing there. And I said "I'm just sitting here thinking about things." He then says, "You have a Fort Rucker sticker on your bumper. We've had a lot of AWOLs from Fort Rucker. You AWOL?" I said, "No it's my dad's car. He just loaned it to me."

This is where I learned not to carry my military ID around with me. He asked for my ID. By then I was in such a panic that I just automatically reached into my pocket and gave him my military ID. I told him that I was on leave. He tells me to come to his squad car and then says he's going to call the coordinating operator officer or something, and they're going to check my story. I was so scared. He asked which company I was in. So I blurted something out which was wrong, because I was so afraid at that point. I was barely able to talk. And he said, "Okay, so you were in this company and you're being sent to Vietnam. We're going to check this out." He's talking to this operator saying, "I got this guy, Joseph B—. He says he was at Fort Ord in this company and he's going to Vietnam." And so we wait, and we wait. And he looks at me and he says, "You know, if you're AWOL, you might as well tell me because we're going to find out." And I'm just sitting there thinking, I'm not gonna say anything. If you're going to catch me, you're gonna have to do it.

It was excruciating waiting. Probably a minute later the officer came back and said, "Yep, he's okay. He checks out." I don't know how, because I had given them erroneous information with regard to which company I was in at Fort Ord. Maybe it was just a big ruse on his part. He was just trying to shake me down. But then he says, "Okay, it is all right, you can go. But you know, you better be careful." I thought, My God, I'm not even out of the country and I'm already caught. That would have been terrible.

My parents told me they [army officials] came pretty much right on the 14th day. God bless my parents, because they had to lie: "Oh, we haven't seen him." My mother was great because she pretended she couldn't speak English that well, which she was very good at doing. They told me later that the weird thing was that they sent the local FBI agent to look for me. And they knew him from church. My dad said it was really awkward to have this guy come, and he was so embarrassed. "Sorry. But I got to say your son's AWOL." They would have to express surprise and they would ask questions, and my mother would pretend like she couldn't understand and couldn't speak. My father had to really act and lie that they had never seen me. But it was difficult. They [the officials] went to see my grandparents, who were living close by, as well. And it was very hard for them. They were kind of shocked. They told me later that FBI and police were coming to their house looking for their grandson. I hadn't told them what I was doing. I didn't want to spread the word. I felt really bad that they had to go through that.

» I didn't know very much about Canada at all. All I knew is that it was north of the United States. So I got on a bus in Dothan, Alabama, and just headed north.

I remember my father said to me, "Look, when you get up to Canada, you're gonna have to try to blend in and look like a Canadian. Because who knows who's going to be looking for you." And he says, "Well, you know, we're gonna go get you a lumberjack jacket because that's what they wear up there." So we went to Sears and got a lumberjack jacket. I had that, a pair of jeans, a change of clothes.

I didn't want to take anything that connected me to the military, and that was a problem because I didn't have any ID. My licence had expired, and it would have been very difficult had I been stopped in the States. All I had was a military ID to show. That would have raised a lot of red flags. So I had my birth certificate for ID, a couple of books, and a map. That's all I took. And I had about $350.

I wound up on the border of New Brunswick and Maine at a place called Houlton, Maine. I checked into a hotel, looked at the map, tried to figure out the best way to get into Canada, and hung around there for a couple of days trying to plot my path and figure out how I was gonna do this. I didn't want to go to the border crossing, because I suspected that they would be looking for me and they would have me on some kind of list or some way to figure out who I was. I wanted to totally avoid that.

Looking at the map, I figured that I could just walk through the forest, cross the border, and then walk over to the highway on the Canadian side and then proceed. I went into the woods. I remember I had been reading *The Sun Also Rises* and reading about Hemingway going out fishing and eating cheese and bread and wine. So I went and I got myself a bottle of Cheez Whiz and some Italian bread and a sleeping bag. I bought a toque and some gloves, and I just headed into the forest.

It was a late winter there, it was April, and there was a lot of snow. It was very slow going. Every time I took a step, the snow would come up to mid-thigh. I trudged through the forest for two and a half days. At night I would take pine boughs and lay them out and then leave a sleeping bag on top and then just go to sleep there. I kept walking and walking and trying to calculate when I would cross the border. I was afraid that maybe they had some kind of tripwires or something to catch people going in illegally. And just having come from the jungles of Vietnam, I was pretty paranoid about tripwires, so I went very slowly.

At one point I stepped on some thin ice and fell into the creek and got all wet, which wasn't good because it was pretty cold. And then, finally, I saw what I thought was the border station. I observed it for a while and saw cars going up to it, stopping, and then continuing, so I figured that that was the border station and figured that I was in Canada. So I walked over to the highway, to where I thought was past the border station, and started hitchhiking, and some guys picked me up. Canadian guys, and I thought, Hey, this is great! They're going to take me to the nearest town and then I'll see what I can do from here. Unfortunately, I had miscalculated. I wasn't in Canada yet. I was still in the States. They turned around this big bend, and they went right smack dab to the border station that I had been looking at. I've always had a terrible sense of direction, and there I was at the Canadian and US border.

The border guard came over and asked all the guys who they were and where they were from, and they all told him they were all Canadians. He looked at me and asked, "Well, who are you? Where are you from?" So I said, "Well, I'm from the States. I'm a student. I'm just travelling and going into Canada to look around. You know, I wanted to take some time off from school and, you know, sort of have an experience." And he asked me how much money I had. I told him and he said, "Well, what are you gonna do when you run out of money?" And I said, "Oh, I'll just get a part-time job or something." That was the wrong answer. He said, "I'm sorry, I can't let you into Canada because you're gonna be taking a job away from a Canadian. Plus you're gonna be working illegally. So I'm going to have to tell you to go back into the States. I'm not going to deport you or anything right now. I'm just telling you not to try to get back in, because I'm going to call all the border stations within five miles of here, and I'm going to tell them who you are and to be on the lookout for you if you try to go through another border station."

I was really disheartened. I had to go back to Maine, back to the hotel. And I thought, What am I gonna do? So I thought I'd try it again. At least now I know for sure where the border station is. So back into the woods, another two and a half days trudging through the snow. This time I got it right. I crossed into Canada, went over to the highway, and totally avoided this border station. I went into the nearest little town, which was Woodstock. It was early in the morning, and I was really hungry. I went into this gas station restaurant. I was sitting there eating breakfast, and I looked up, and who comes in through the doors for breakfast but the border guard. I thought, Oh my God, he's going to see me, and I'm done. Fortunately, there was a back door. I just put some money on the table, snuck out the back door, and went out to the highway. He never saw me, which was a real surprise to me because I was wearing exactly the same clothes. I was wearing my lumberjack jacket.

I went out to the road, hitchhiked, and a guy picked me up. He drove me to Fredericton, New Brunswick. I was so ignorant of Canada. He was about my age and he was telling me he worked for the Ministry of Transport, building roads. And I asked him, "Well, how'd you get out of the draft?" He looked at me and said, "We don't have a draft. This is Canada." And I thought, Okay, this is great. I didn't know that.

I stayed in Fredericton for about three weeks, working odd jobs, painting apartments for a while. But I just couldn't get ahead. I was just breaking even. Having lived in Los Angeles for so long, I was used to big cities, and I felt more confident being able to get a job in a big city. I decided to go to Toronto, because one day I was watching television and I saw a program about a guy named Bill Spira, who was in Toronto and helping deserters and dodgers regularize their status. So I thought, Well, this is good for me. I'm sure I'll be able to get a job in a big city and I'll meet this guy and he's gonna help me get legal in Canada.

I didn't have a clue. I was just an ignorant young man, just scrambling. I had confidence that I would be able to figure it out. So I got on a bus. I arrived at the Toronto bus station at Dundas and Bay. It was raining really hard, and I went into the station, bought a newspaper, and looked for a place to stay. I saw an ad for a rooming house in Downsview, a long ways away from Dundas and Bay. But I didn't know that. I called them up and I said, "I'm coming." So I got into a cab and we drove and drove and finally we got there. And I went in and it was full of Newfoundlanders, which was a fantastic thing. They were a great introduction to Canada, but I couldn't understand what they were saying. They were so friendly though. So I felt really good. But embarrassed, because I had to keep asking them what they were saying. And so finally I said to them, "Where are you guys from? Are you Canadian?" And they looked at me and said, "We're from Newfoundland." And they said, "It's part of Canada."

I got a part-time job working at Dominion grocery store, because I had been a grocery clerk in Los Angeles. I was a hard worker and I did well at Dominion. But they could only offer me part-time work. So again I was just able to break even. I was at a mall and I saw an ad for full-time staff at Food City, a new grocery chain. So I applied. They gave me a full-time job, and it paid really well.

I worked at the Food City on Eglinton Avenue, five miles from the boarding house where I was living. It was great. I'd just take the bus. I worked the midnight shift, and they paid me enough money that I was able to save in order to go to school. Because by then I had decided that I had to go to school.

But I still had the problem of regularizing my status. I was still illegal in Canada. And I was working illegally. So I went to the immigration authorities to ask them: "How do I become a permanent resident?" They told me, "You have to get a letter promising you a job, and you have to have $150. And then you have to apply and pass the requirements." So I asked my employer for a letter and I told them, "Please give me a letter saying that you're offering me a job." They gave me a letter that said I had already been working here. I looked at the letter and thought, This is gonna be a problem. But I was afraid to ask them to correct it, basically asking them to lie. So I didn't. I thought, I'm just going to take my chances.

The immigration office in downtown Toronto told me that I could make my application there, but it would take about three months. If I wanted to get my permanent residency status quicker, I should go to the border, because they could give it to me on the same day. Things were much different then. I went to the Rainbow Bridge, Niagara Falls. I had my letter, my $150. I walked into the border station. They asked me where I was coming from. And I said "Toronto." And they told me if I'm applying for landed immigrant status, I have to come right across from the States: "You can't just come right from Canada if you're doing this at the border." They said, "You can go apply in Toronto if you want." But I had already done that and decided to do it at the border. There was no way I was going back into the States because I thought that as soon as I crossed the border, they would have me on a list. I was so afraid that they would catch me. I just went behind the border station, had a cigarette, and waited for a while.

Then I noticed where people were walking across the bridge. I kind of went over into that area and then kind of joined in with other people walking across the bridge to try to make it look like I was coming from the States. And it worked. I went in and they interviewed me. But when they looked at my letter, they got really upset because I had already been working. They told me, "You've been working illegally in Canada. This is not right. You're not even accepted as a resident and you're already breaking the law." The officer that interviewed me was an older gentleman who was really angry with me. Fortunately, some of his co-workers were younger and more sympathetic to me. They took him aside, talked to him for a while, and then he came back and he said, "All right, I'm going to make an exception, but don't break any more laws. You know, I could easily just send you right back right now to the States." He gave me a good dressing-down, but that was okay. I understood that this was just what he had to do.

They gave me my landed status and certificate right then and there on July 14, 1969, which was my 22nd birthday. I was very happy. I came back to Toronto, continued to work, saved my money, and went to York University in 1971.

After getting my BA, I started law school in 1973 and got married right before starting law school. I graduated from law school in 1976, then articled for a year and got called to the bar in 1978. My first wife and I divorced in 1978 after I was called to the bar.

I had to become a citizen to be called to the bar. That was a bit of a harrowing experience because it was 1975 and I didn't know how I was going to become a citizen. I was unsure about whether I could be a dual citizen. I wrestled with the idea of giving up my American citizenship. I thought maybe I would have to do that. As it turned out, I didn't have to give it up because Canada recognizes multiple citizenships. So I became a Canadian citizen and was able to be called to the bar.

As a lawyer, I helped to counsel some deserters and dodgers. Most of the people that we worked with were from Parkdale. In those days there were some strong organizations in Toronto that were counselling draft dodgers and deserters. The Toronto Anti-Draft Programme was one of them. It seemed to me that they had enough resources to counsel almost all of the deserters and dodgers that wanted their help. I think most of the deserters and dodgers gravitated towards them for that reason, so they didn't come to Parkdale legal services. But I did counsel some draft dodgers and deserters that had gone to the Quakers.

I practised in Toronto for about four years and then accepted a job in the Arctic on Baffin Island. I moved there with my second wife, and I worked for an Inuit legal services centre called Maliiganik Tukisiiniakvik. I was the only lawyer in the Baffin region. There were about 10,000 people on Baffin Island. It was a wonderful experience. My two children were born there. After four years I decided that it was time to leave. I took a sabbatical and we all went to France for a year. I wanted to learn French. My father was living in Germany, so I wanted to spend time with him too.

After a year we came back to Toronto, and I started working for the Ministry of the Attorney General and with Indigenous persons in northern Ontario. I worked there for two years and then applied to become a judge. I was accepted and I was appointed to the bench on December 31, 1989. I was a judge of the Ontario Court of Justice for 32 years.

» I integrated into Canadian society by starting to work and getting to know people, making some friends, then by going to university and starting to slowly just become part of Canadian society. When I first got here, I didn't tell anybody that I was a deserter because that was before I was granted landed immigrant status and I was really afraid. I didn't know if somebody would report me or not. I made some friends that I really liked, and yet I was holding back this big secret and I felt really bad about it. But then, slowly but surely, I started to realize I was going to be okay here. Even before I got my landed immigrant status, I just knew it. I could feel it. And then I started telling people that I was a deserter. I found that 99 percent of Canadians accepted me wholeheartedly. They thought the war in Vietnam was wrong. They understood and were very supportive. And I'll forever be thankful.

I've always been really grateful to the Canadian government because they allowed me to be here even though I was a deserter from the American army. I'd always mention this to my third wife. And she encouraged me to write a letter to Pierre Trudeau, who was the prime minister when I came to Canada, because I'd always told her that I was so thankful. I thought, He's not going to pay attention to a letter from some puny little judge in Toronto. But I followed her advice and I wrote him a letter, giving him a very brief synopsis of who I was and what I'd done and how grateful I was, and I thanked him. And he wrote back! He thanked me for the letter and congratulated me "for serving Canada so well." It meant a lot to me. I still have the letter, framed. It gave me a sense of closure.

» I had a lot of baggage when I got here. I was very angry. I felt that I had been given two choices by the American government: go to war and help kill people, or go to jail. I tried to apply for conscientious objector status, but my draft board turned me down. I told them I was Catholic. They said, "Well, you know, there's nothing in the Catholic religion that says anything is wrong with killing." I was shocked at that because the sixth Commandment does say do not kill. Nevertheless, they turned me down. So those were my two options: go to jail or go to war. Or a third option: leave the country. But I wound up going to Vietnam, trying to rationalize my way through it. I saw what the horror of war was. I saw how all the

American institutions had basically lied: the educational institutions, the government, and even the Catholic Church.

After I refused to go on line any longer, they sent me to talk to a priest, who was encouraging me to go back out on line and kill Vietnamese because "If we don't kill them, they're going to kill all the Catholics. Because they're all communists." It was shocking, because I truly believe in Christ, and in his message, which is a non-violent one. The advice that I was getting from priests in Vietnam was completely contradictory. I felt betrayed by the Catholic Church, the government, and the educational institutions, who had always told me how great America was and how we were always on the right side and we always fought for freedom and always defended people. I saw what the American army was doing there. I saw other people blown apart: kids, old people, old villagers. They were killing a lot of villagers that weren't doing anything wrong. And it went on and on. War just completely corrupts everything.

Once I got to Canada, I was carrying all that around with me, and I was very angry. Also, I missed all my friends. I thought, Well this is it. I'm never gonna be able to go back to the United States. I'm coming to a country where I knew not one person. Plus, I had the trauma of actually having been in combat as a medic. How to deal with that? And just the general insecurity that created in me.

I didn't handle it that well. I frequently vented my anger verbally with my friends. Thank God for them, because they put up with me. At every party, every get-together, I would always turn the conversation to the war in Vietnam. I'm sure I became very tiresome and tedious to my friends, but they all stuck by me. But it's so hard...I couldn't get rid of it. And then one day I realized, Well, either I let this go, or it's going to wind up being very harmful to me in the long run. And so, thank God, I was able to somehow let most of it go. A lot of it stayed, but I let enough of it go that it wasn't interfering with my life, it wasn't destroying me. And I was no longer inflicting it upon my friends, because I realized, This is enough, I have to stop doing this. This is not helping—because I wasn't feeling any better. Even when I was angry, I wasn't feeling any better. There was never a relief. So I thought, There's got to be some other kind of relief here. I've got to do something.

One thing that really helped me was I started training in karate. And I had a wonderful, brilliant teacher. He would assess every student. He knew us better than we knew ourselves, our capabilities, how far to push us. I trained in karate for about 20 years, became a black belt. The training was tough, but that's what I needed to channel my anger. And I wasn't going around beating people up, that wasn't part of our training. The training was so hard that it helped me to exorcise the anger that I had. Because when I got really angry, I was just trying harder. And that really helped me tremendously.

I've always tried to be a spiritual person. You know, I prayed and I tried to have a strong spiritual practice. I believe in God. I know Buddhists don't believe in God, but I practise Buddhism as well. But I sincerely think my faith in God and Christ and my Buddhist practice have all combined to help me a lot, to be able to not only deal with all that baggage, but also to express it and get it out of me and to understand it.

One of the most important things that happened to me to be able to deal with it is my third wife. She told me that I needed to go back to Vietnam. I was having recurring nightmares ever since I left Vietnam. I was really afraid to go back because I thought that I would have a nervous breakdown, that I would totally freak out once I was back there. But she encouraged me. She said, "No, it's going to be good for you." I was really afraid, but I thought, Okay, I'll go anyway. So we went. This was shortly after they opened their doors to tourism, maybe 1997. We started in Hanoi, that forbidden place that I always heard about. And then we worked our way south down to what is now called Ho Chi Minh City. I saw a lot of the ruins from the war, interacted with the people, and I realized that the Vietnamese seem to have gotten over it and they were getting on with their lives. That taught me a lot. And I thought, Wow, if they can get over it and get on with their lives, well, I surely should be able to. So I learned a lot from their example. They were very kind, very friendly, helpful. There were some that I ran into that gave me some hard looks. But I can totally understand that.

The most important moment in the whole thing was when we got down to Ho Chi Minh City and I went to Củ Chi, which was the base in the rear that I was assigned to, after I got deployed to the jungle. And I saw all the old buildings that were crumbling. They'd not been maintained. And it became a metaphor for me. And I thought, Yes, you know, I'm...That's the era that I'm still living in, mentally. But it's over. It's something that you can let go of. And so it worked. I maybe have had one or two nightmares since then, and that's it. All of that has combined to help me deal with the baggage.

I've also been very fortunate in my work. I was accepted to law school, which meant so much to me. To me it symbolized acceptance by Canada, that they would accept me to be a lawyer. So that really helped me. And it gave me encouragement for the future. It showed me that, yes, I was going to be able to make something of myself here. I was gonna be able to contribute and give back to society. And I had a wonderful time practising. I had a great practice. I got to go to the Arctic. And I felt that that was really helping people there. The Inuit offered me a job. They said, "We need you, come help us." I thought it was fantastic. So all that had a healing effect.

And then when I got accepted, appointed as a judge. Oh my God! I thought, Wow, this society really is accepting me. And I'm just forever humbled and grateful.

I've had a wonderful career as a judge. I've travelled all over Canada. I've sat in Indigenous communities in the far north of Ontario. All of this has had a tremendous healing effect for me. And I'm no longer really angry. Probably there's still some anger there somewhere. But it's not a problem. I've really come to terms with it, and I'm very happy. I've never regretted my decision to come to Canada, not even for a nanosecond. Never.

And the way things turned out after I deserted, the more that became known about what the American government was doing in Vietnam in those years, the more I felt that my decision was the correct one. Especially when it came out how the American government lied to the American people. The Pentagon Papers came out. I saw the documentary *The Fog of War*, in which Robert McNamara, one of the main architects of the Vietnam war, said that he is proud of his accomplishments but is sorry for the errors that he committed. In his book *In Retrospect*, he said that he felt guilty and regretful for the mistakes that he made in orchestrating the war. So I feel that my decision was not only correct morally, but it was correct factually, if I can put it that way. All of that has combined to really heal me.

I'm very fortunate to have been married to my third wife, who really understood me and never pushed me about Vietnam. I knew that she appreciated how I felt about it. And that was always great. In addition to encouraging me to return to Vietnam, she facilitated my reunion with the doctor and medic who helped me get out of Saigon. This reunion and the return to Vietnam helped me tremendously to alleviate the trauma.

My past influences my work because I understand to a great extent the plight of many immigrants who come before me, having committed a crime for one reason or another. Many of them are in great distress because they're immigrants. They're having a hard time adjusting to Canadian society. I did a lot of work in immigration law when I was a lawyer. And we have many people that come before us as judges who have immigration difficulties. I can relate to that. The circumstances are different. But it does give me an understanding of the great pressures on immigrants, and a lot of them buckle under the pressure. Unfortunately, sometimes they turn to crime, get addicted to drugs, and act out in other criminal ways. I feel that having gone through what I went through, I have some measure of understanding of them that I wouldn't have had otherwise. I know that many of their situations are really different from what mine was, but there's still a general feeling there. So it has helped me a lot.

As far as my status in the States goes, in 1974 Gerald Ford was president, and he established an amnesty program for Vietnam-era deserters and draft dodgers. But there was another procedure called a Chapter 10 discharge. I don't know for sure why the American government established this program, but I think that they did it because they just wanted to close the file on all of these guys who deserted and dodged the draft. And they wanted to extend or amplify this program that was designed to deal with persons who were just incompatible with the army: people that went AWOL all the time, people that had psychiatric problems, people that got into fights with their officers, that type of situation. But it required that you go back to the States and turn yourself in. And I was really afraid to do that.

I met a woman who worked for the Quakers in Toronto. She told me about a program that the Quakers were running in conjunction with this Ford amnesty program. And the plan was that I would go to Fort Dix, which is where I would have to turn myself in. I would report to the office

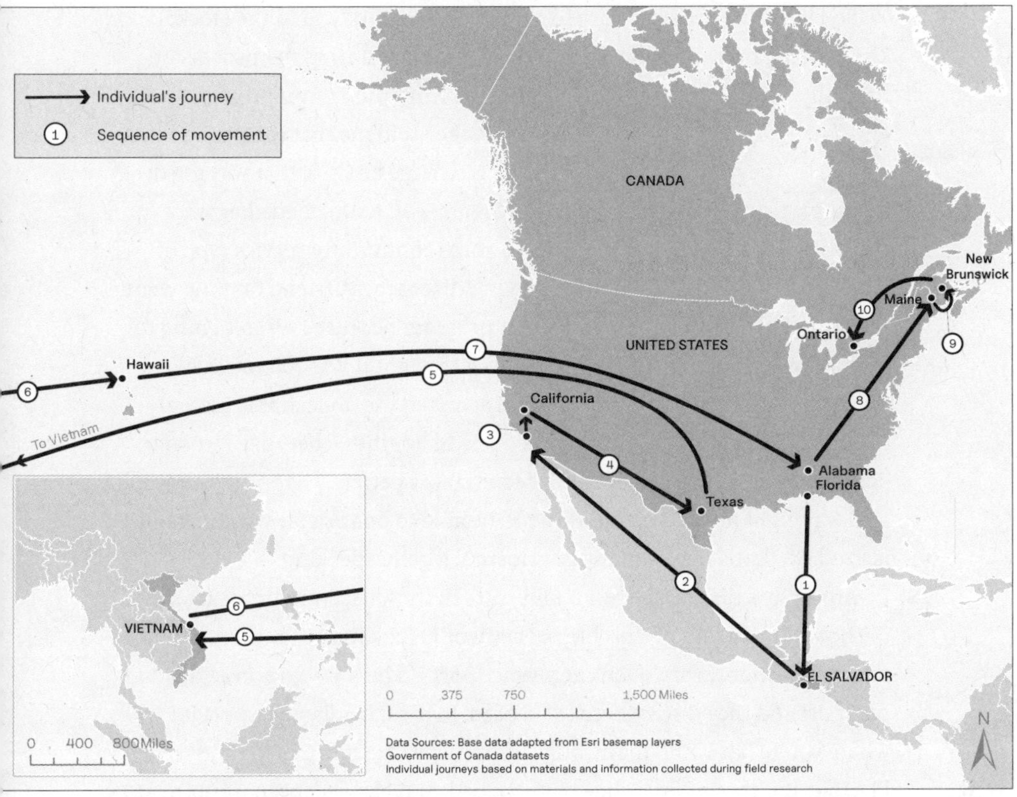

MAP 5: Joe's journey from 1947 to 1969.

of the Quakers. And they would take my name and write down the date that I went into Fort Dix to turn myself in. They would monitor my case and make sure that I got out of there as planned according to this Chapter 10 Discharge Program. They told me that if I didn't come out in a few days, they would start asking questions.

They assured me that they had done this for others and it had worked, and that they had been able to come back to Canada. So I thought it was worth it to try. I had confidence in the Quakers. And I knew that if I let the chance go by, that I probably would never be able to go back to the States. My parents still lived in the States then. And I thought it would be a good idea at least to have the ability to go back there if I wanted, not to live, but to just travel and visit my parents. They were getting older and couldn't keep coming up to Canada.

So I went to Fort Dix. I turned myself in. They put you in the stockade. They cut my hair. Gave me the uniform. And they started the process of basically administratively discharging me from the army. And after two and a half days of being in the stockade, they told me that the process was complete. They gave me an undesirable discharge because that was the deal. If you participated in the amnesty program, you reaffirmed allegiance to the United States and promised to do some community service type of work, and they would give you a general discharge. A friend of mine went through that. I didn't go through that program because I wasn't going to reaffirm allegiance to the United States. I thought it was too much like saying I was sorry. I wasn't sorry. And I accepted the undesirable discharge. It wasn't going to harm my job prospects or anything, because I wasn't going to be looking for a job in the States. I was perfectly happy in Canada. And I thought it was a useful thing to be able to do to get my status regularized. So that's how I finally got closure, legally speaking.

After I was discharged, for a few years in the '70s, every time I crossed the border I had a bit of a problem. They would look me up and they would ask me questions. They'd look at my passport. I'd be travelling on a Canadian passport and they'd see where I was born. In the Canadian passport it says where you're born. And they would ask me why I went to Canada and things like that. But then after a while that stopped. And I haven't been troubled at all for years and years. So that worked out well for me as well.

I identify as both American and Canadian. I lived a lot of my formative years in the United States. I also lived a lot of my formative years in El Salvador. So I identify a bit as a Latin American, American, and Canadian. I always wonder what it means to be Canadian. I have a lot of friends who were born here. And I notice that there is a bit of a difference between us. I don't share the same cultural references and same cultural experiences. I can barely skate. I've never played hockey. So there are those kind of differences. But they are minimal. And I guess I don't know which label to put on myself, but if I had to, I'd put those three labels on me. Part of me does feel American when I meet another American. I instantly feel some kind of connection to them. It's not a conscious thing that happens, it just happens. And so that to me means that, yes, part of me is still very much American. But I feel like I'm all three, because I have a very strong Latin American side as well, and I have a lot of Latin American friends.

14 Reflections

The Courage to Resist

THE COURAGE TO RESIST begins with the imagination. To fight for a different life, we must imagine a different world. To resist war is to imagine freedom—freedom from violence. Although Canada does not always offer such refuge, freedom is imagined and hoped for as a space of possibility. These are myths that the contributors to this book contend with, and notions of Canada as safe haven for which we all struggle.

Each personal history in this book conveys commonalities that connect people in their search for a better life and a peaceful future that includes freedom from war. Like all people seeking asylum, war resisters share universal needs for freedom, for refuge. These stories are, therefore, not only about resisting war, but also about supporting both people seeking asylum and people who came to Canada with refugee status, so many of whom are displaced by war, whether as civilians or as soldiers fleeing violence. The stories shared in this collection offer reminders that governments and their public policies, along with activists and their campaigns for social justice, play profound roles in people's everyday lives.

The different political and cultural landscapes in which each generation arrived during the wars in Vietnam, Iraq, and Afghanistan show how Canada has changed over the decades between these arrivals. It is too easy to forget histories of refuge, to forget those who were excluded, and to forget the important role that Canada has played—and can play—in the world as a haven from war-making. This role matters profoundly, existing at the heart of the myths and realities of Canada as a safe haven, an ideal that we must fight for in any political moment.

Today, border crossings into Canada from the United States remain highly politicized, and legal struggles in Canadian courts and challenges to the Safe Third Country Agreement (STCA) continue as I write. Since its inception in 2004, the STCA between Canada and the US restricts the rights of asylum seekers, requiring people with access to asylum systems in the first country they pass through to remain there, rather than cross into another country. While the STCA has exceptions and legal and geographical complications, it has become a legal battleground, and a rallying cry for those who seek to protect humans and human rights, and for those who seek to restrict access to the refugee claimant system in Canada (Rehaag & Aiken 2020). The STCA is part of a broader global trend to restrict paths to political asylum (Mountz 2020a) and is at the centre of the latest round of exclusion from and restricted access to asylum in Canada.

Changes in policy and practice continued along the border at the heart of the stories in this book, including a major expansion of the STCA in 2023 that promised severe and blanket restrictions to access for anyone crossing the land border to seek asylum. Previously, if people crossed the border in between official crossings, their claims for asylum were heard. The 2023 amendment extended the application of the STCA across time and space, along the full extent of the border. People who crossed between official entry points would now be returned per the original terms of the agreement if they were caught making an asylum claim within 14 days of their entry. This policy was challenged in court, where policymakers, lawmakers, refugee advocates, and activists fought to turn back the new geographical and legal grounds that extend policing of the border and restrict access to a chance at refuge.

» Each history in this collection provides insight into the complexities and idiosyncrasies of sojourns across borders. These are stories shot through with emotion and conflict as individuals explain how they struggled to make life-altering decisions and create new lives in Canada. I are honoured to have had the privilege to hear, document, and share these stories, effectively telling them back to their authors and then to broader audiences. I admire the courage that our storytellers have shown, not only in resisting war and standing up for what they believe. I find inspiration in the courage they have shown in sharing the intimacies of their journeys, hope and comfort in their survival.

One theme recurring across these stories is that of movement, a life in motion. People who enlisted or were drafted were trained as soldiers and ordered into wars in faraway places, only to then flee home to forge a life in a new country. There, these experiences of moving from place to place often continued in the work of settling and establishing a life and alternative communities in a new society, whether in Canada's largest cities or the farthest-flung corners of the Maritime provinces or the Gulf Islands of British Columbia.

I discovered other patterns working across these histories, such as the frequent story of military recruiters locating and programming very young adults who have not yet figured out their futures, including how to pay for university or shelter. Resisters speak frequently and bitterly of this fundamental deception, of trying to do the job that they were promised in their efforts to stay out of direct combat and in their attempts to find principled positions within the chaos of war.

There are also significant differences between resisters—people who faced racism in their journeys and on return, the gendering of experiences, class differences, and how access, or a lack of access, to resources can make each stage of migration a little easier or more difficult. Details that once seemed mundane, or even accidental, prove centrally important to the outcomes of these cross-border histories of war resistance.

Individuals, families, and communities carry the intergenerational burdens of war as families struggle with the intimate aftermath of trauma and its negative effects on the mental health and well-being of the people they share homes and relationships with. I often heard histories of military families, with sons following in their fathers' footsteps when they had not had the opportunity to really know their father—as in Robin's desire to get to know his biological father better by serving in the military.

What resisters hold in common across generations are experiences of post-traumatic stress disorder, which permeate these histories and lives, but are often not spoken of. In listening to these oral histories, the pervasive traumas were often experienced and felt affectively in silences rather than in words spoken. I sought ways to point out, where appropriate, how trauma itself shaped lives, shaped who survives on these pages, whose stories are told, by whom, and in what ways.

These struggles with mental health and well-being make it even more challenging for resisters to continue to show courage and stand up for moral standpoints that challenge mainstream culture and belief systems operating in the haze of militarism. Resisters continue to battle in their decision to break ranks with a conformist society shaped by militarism. For their nonconformity, they have been shamed by families, peers, and community members, often with enormous and lasting personal implications.

» With the exception of Esther's husband, Dave, who died of cancer in 2020, and Lee, who died in 2024 as this collection was completed, the storytellers remain very much alive and thriving. They continue to explore the world as adventurers and activists, and readers might enjoy updates on where they are now in their lives.

Esther misses Dave each day, but lives a full life travelling the world as an activist with Christian Peacemakers. She frequents destinations such as Palestine and the Mexico–US borderlands, carrying out her activist work and lifelong commitment to peace and social justice.

Robin has lived in many sites around the US since his return from Canada, including California, Washington, and Colorado. He has worked in massage, education, and the cannabis industry, and sees each line of work as crucial to human healing and well-being.

Linjamin travelled to Russia, not long after completing this oral history, in order to marry his Russian girlfriend. They remained in Russia during the pandemic, eventually leaving just as Russia and Ukraine went to war. They travelled across Latin America with hopes of settling in North America, which they did when the opportunity arrived.

Leah continues to work and live as a very active community leader in the Slocan Valley. Neil and John S. also lead active lives in their small western communities.

Michelle remains a lifelong activist and community leader, campaigning tirelessly and fiercely for social justice from her home base in Toronto. While the War Resisters Support Campaign she co-founded ended in 2019, her work on other campaigns continues.

During the global pandemic that started in 2020, Corey and his partner moved to the remote woods of the Maritimes, more than 100 kilometres from the nearest town.

Lee, in contrast, remained a lifelong resident and community activist in downtown Toronto, but for his annual travels to Vietnam.

John F. and Joe also remain in Toronto, where each enjoys an active life following recent retirements. Joe has since learned how to skate and can be found playing hockey, a beloved Canadian pastime that he had not learned as a kid growing up in El Salvador and the United States.

Dean completed his education at Fleming College in Peterborough, where he lives with his partner and sons.

People often ask if it was a challenge to get people to participate in oral histories. There were certainly people who declined the request to record an oral history and to participate in the documentary film *Safe Haven*. However, I am grateful to the vast majority who chose to take part.

When my collaborators and I organized workshops and film screenings, the two generations of resisters were able to meet and get to know each other, as did many in the Campaign. These connections across generations have been healing and affirmative.

I was also fortunate to work with Corey as second camera on *Safe Haven*. Corey's presence and demeanour helped us to build relations of trust, support, deep empathy, and understanding with participants.

We were also fortunate to build relationships through collaboration with the War Resisters Support Campaign, and worked together to build an archive of the Campaign, preserved and memorialized for later generations. This curated archive will be housed at the University of Toronto's Special Collections, alongside the archives of the Toronto Anti-Draft Programme. In assembling this archive collaboratively with members of the Campaign, we were united in the belief that US cycles of war-making will continue, and that future generations will learn from the political lessons of this campaign for social justice and for the right to stay in Canada, just as this campaign learned from the generation of activists who fought for safe haven during the earlier conflict in Vietnam.

» This book contributes to the crucial collective project of documenting and remembering histories of war, migration, and displacement.

As I write, the world has been contending with over three years of war on Ukraine by Russia, with an escalation that began in February 2022 and came to involve countries around the world, including the United States and Canada, deciding how they will participate and support remotely. The stories in this book have told us that war has devastating consequences, including displacement, tearing apart families, and uprooting lives. The war between Russia and Ukraine has included forced conscription of men in both countries, reigniting debate about their opportunities to flee as a strategy of resisting war.

It is troubling to recognize the cycle of war as it appears in the present moment. The US is always funding war somewhere; this is not a unique moment historically. It is a rehearsal of similar players, strategies, contentions, and justifications for war-making, with disregard for people who actively carry out the work of these wars and the consequences that await them and their families. The war in Ukraine presents an opportune moment to talk about the many costs of war and forced conscription, which has happened in both Russia and Ukraine. It is imperative to talk about what happens to people who are forced to fight in wars, and about those who resist, at immense personal costs. Wars in Ukraine and Gaza also provide an opportunity to talk about trauma and the distress to physical and mental health experienced by those who live in conflict zones and by people who actively participate in wars. The war also makes it more important than ever to talk about civilian deaths, displacement, and the millions of refugees produced, and about whether and where people are able to find safe haven.

Wealthy countries of the Global North continue to be complicit in war-making, not acknowledging that the fallout of these wars creates issues they themselves have to contend with, especially the issue of refugees and displacement. War-making countries too often place the blame on people fleeing these violent spaces as a fundamental matter of survival.

It is striking that Prime Minister Pierre Trudeau remains revered among the earlier generation of war resisters, who were grateful for a government that took a stand against US militarism, even when some 12,000 Canadian soldiers also fought in the war in Vietnam alongside American soldiers. All the more striking is the fact that the government of his son, Prime Minister Justin Trudeau, chose to accept a very small number of the next generation of American war resisters and did so quietly. This contrast reflects the broader shift in Canada's political landscape that informs the outcome of the war resisters' search for safe haven. Whereas the earlier generation admired Pierre Trudeau and benefitted from his overt assertion of Canadian sovereignty and humanitarian ideals during the Vietnam War, the more recent resisters found cautious, diplomatically constrained responses in the post-9/11 era (Grünendahl 2022).

These histories of war resistance are of national and global importance. As war rages on around the globe, we must continue to reflect on what kind of safe haven Canada has been, historically, for war resisters, and ask what kind of safe haven it might be in the future, not only for people from the United States, but for all people who resist war and arrive in search of refuge. As the contributors to this book demonstrate, this question must be asked by each generation and can never be taken for granted.

To this end, *Crossing into Canada* is one part of a commitment to collectively document and share these war resister histories with as many people as possible. We must continue a sustained dialogue about the costs and consequences of war, which are ultimately human, intimate experiences of violence and trauma. If we do not contend with histories of war, history repeats. This commitment has driven our collaboration with the WRSC, with a resolve to archive and forge creative ways to remember and discuss.

As activist and campaign leader Michelle Robidoux said, "These are conversations we need to have if we want to live in a different type of society." This book joins in these dialogues in solidarity, with the hope of facilitating conversations among resisters and readers. As a queer immigrant who came to Canada in search of a different life, I join in solidarity with resisters in the desire to live in, talk about, and collectively build a society that safeguards freedom.

» As I completed final work on this book, US citizens voted former president Donald Trump back into office, this time with Republicans controlling the House of Representatives and the Senate, amid a wave of violent, racist, and xenophobic rhetoric dedicated to the closure and militarization of borders. Safe haven once again came under severe threat in the United States, and those seeking safety will once again look north, as they did in the months and years following Trump's first election in 2016.

Wars in Ukraine and Palestine rage on, including the humanitarian disaster of over 80,000 deaths in Gaza (Fieldhouse 2025), unleashing prolonged conflict in the present and the threat of new wars that will come in the future.

Geopolitical relations entered yet another round of uncertainty, with Russia and China seen more favourably by Trump, and Americans at risk of losing respect and long-standing allies around the world. This includes a new round of uncertainty in the geopolitical relationship between Canada and the United States.

The journey to safe haven is far more perilous as I complete this book than it was when I began, a devastating reality that serves as a reminder that rights to freedom and mobility, and the right to live free from war, can never be taken for granted. The campaign to support war resisters is part of a larger movement to support all people displaced by war and searching for refuge and a life free from war. To live in peace, we must imagine and work towards peaceful futures together.

References and Additional Reading

Associated Press. (2007, June 28). Military makes little effort to punish deserters: Although numbers rising, only 5 percent of lawbreakers reprimanded. *NBC News*. http://www.nbcnews.com/id/19489285/ns/us_newsmilitary/t/military-makes-little-effort-punish-deserters/#.VCwhQWBL09Q

Bailey, B. (2009). *America's army: Making the all-volunteer force.* Harvard University Press.

Bailey, B., & Immerman, R.H. (Eds.). (2015). *Understanding the US wars in Iraq and Afghanistan.* NYU Press.

Bibbings, L. (2003). Images of manliness: The portrayal of soldiers and conscientious objectors in the Great War. *Social & Legal Studies, 12*(3), 335–358.

Campbell, L., Dawson, M., & Gidney, C. (Eds.). (2015). *Worth fighting for: Canada's tradition of war resistance from 1812 to the War on Terror.* Between the Lines.

Churchill, D.S. (2004). An ambiguous welcome: Vietnam draft resistance, the Canadian state, and Cold War containment. *Histoire sociale/Social History, 37*(73), 1–26.

Corday, C. (2015, November 11). Lost to history: The Canadians who fought in Vietnam. *CBC News*. https://www.cbc.ca/news/canada/british-columbia/lost-to-history-the-canadians-who-fought-in-vietnam-1.3304440

Fieldhouse, R. (2025). First independent survey of deaths in Gaza reports more than 80,000 fatalities. *Nature, 643*(8071): 311–312. doi: 10.1038/d41586-025-02009-8.

Frutkin, M. (2008). *Erratic north: A Vietnam draft resister's life in the Canadian bush.* Dundurn Press.

Grünendahl, S.J. (2022). *US war resisters' quest for refuge in Canada: A comparative study of Vietnam and Afghanistan/Iraq War resisters' migration experiences.* Springer Nature.

Hagan, J. (2001a). Cause and country: The politics of ambivalence and the American Vietnam War resistance in Canada. *Social Problems, 48*(2), 168–184.

Hagan, J. (2001b). *Northern passage: American Vietnam War resisters in Canada.* Harvard University Press.

Haig-Brown, A. (1996). *Hell no, we won't go: Vietnam draft resisters in Canada.* Raincoast Books.

Hipworth, S., & Stewart, L. (Eds.). (2016). *Let them stay: U.S. war resisters in Canada 2004–2016.* Iguana Books.

Hylton, W. (2015, February 25). American deserter. *New York Magazine.* https://nymag.com/intelligencer/2015/02/american-military-deserters-canada.html

Iraq Veterans Against War. (2008). *Warrior writers re-making sense.* L. Brown & Sons Printing.

Iraq Veterans Against War, & Glantz, A. (2008). *Winter soldier, Iraq and Afghanistan: Eyewitness accounts of the occupations.* Haymarket Books.

Jamail, D. (2016). *The will to resist: Soldiers who refuse to fight in Iraq and Afghanistan.* Haymarket Books.

Kasinsky, R.G. (1976). *Refugees from militarism: Draft-age Americans in Canada.* Transaction Books.

Kauffman, G. (2015, July 12). Canada cools to resisters of US's Iraq War: What's changed since Vietnam? *The Christian Science Monitor.* https://www.csmonitor.com/USA/USA-Update/2015/0712/Canada-cools-to-resisters-of-US-s-Iraq-War.-What-s-changed-since-Vietnam

Key, J. (with Hill, L.). (2007). *The deserter's tale: The story of an ordinary soldier who walked away from the war in Iraq.* House of Anansi.

Kurschinski, K. (2010). The true north strong and free: Vietnam War resisters, Canada, and the search for identity, 1964–1974. *The Mirror, 30*(1), 77–98.

Maxwell, D.W. (2006). Religion and politics at the border: Canadian church support for American Vietnam War resisters. *Journal of Church and State*, 48(4), 807–829.

Midwest Committee for Draft Counselling. (n.d.). *Pre-Counsellor curriculum.* Pocock Memorial Collection (MS Coll 331, Box 5, File 3). Thomas Fisher Rare Book Library, Toronto, Canada.

Mountz, A. (2020a). *The death of asylum: Hidden geographies of the enforcement archipelago.* University of Minnesota Press.

Mountz, A. (2020b). Seeking status, forging refuge: US war resister migrations to Canada. *Refuge*, 36(1), 97–107.

Mountz, A., Micieli-Voutsinas, J., & Mohan, S.S. (2022). Contrapuntal histories of war resistance: Mapping US war resister migrations, questioning Canada as safe haven. *The Canadian Geographer/Le Géographe canadien*, 66(4), 741–755.

Ngo, A. (2016). "Journey to Freedom Day Act": The making of the Vietnamese subject in Canada and the erasure of the Vietnam War. *Canadian Review of Social Policy*, 75, 59–86.

Otterman, S. (2005, February 3). Iraq: U.S. deployments at the war's height. Council on Foreign Relations. https://www.cfr.org/backgrounder/iraq-us-deployments-wars-height

Rehaag, S., & Aiken, S. (2020, July 24). Canadian court correctly finds the U.S. is unsafe for refugees. *The Conversation*. https://theconversation.com/canadian-court-correctly-finds-the-u-s-is-unsafe-for-refugees-143239

Ridgley, J. (2011). Refuge, refusal, and acts of holy contagion: The city as a sanctuary for soldiers resisting the Vietnam War. ACME, 10(2), 189–214.

Ruder, E., & Smith, A. (2008). Putting the war on trial: IVAW's new winter soldier hearings in Washington. *International Socialist Review*, 59 (May–June), https://isreview.org/issues/59/rep-wintersoldier/

Satin, M. (2017). *Manual for draft-age immigrants to Canada.* House of Anansi Press. (Original work published 1968)

Sharpless, Rebecca. (2006). The history of oral history. In Thomas Charlton, Lois Myers, & Rebecca Sharpless, eds., *The handbook of oral history*. AltaMira.

Squires, J. (2013). *Building sanctuary: The movement to support Vietnam War resisters in Canada, 1965–1973.* UBC Press.

Steiner, S. (2007). Alternative service or alternative resistance? A Vietnam War draft resister in Canada. *Journal of Mennonite Studies*, 25, 195–204.

Stewart, L. (2018). "Hell, they're your problem, not ours": Draft dodgers, military deserters and Canada-United States relations in the Vietnam War era. *Études canadiennes/Canadian Studies*, 85, 67–96. https://doi.org/10.4000/eccs.1479

Toronto Daily Star. (1970, March 21). PM sees Canada as youth haven from "militarism," 1, 3.

Trudeau, J. [@JustinTrudeau]. (2017, January 1). *Canada strongly condemns today's terrorist attack in Istanbul. We mourn with Turkey, and offer our condolences to the victims' families* [Tweet]. Twitter. https://x.com/JustinTrudeau/status/815684474394578944

Weedon, G. (2014). Military resisters, war resistance, and the ethics of exposure and disclosure. *Cultural Studies? Critical Methodologies*, 14(5), 438–450.

Whitman-Bradley, B., Lezare, S., & Whitman-Bradley, C. (2011). *About Face: Military resisters turn against war. Voices from the Courage to Resist project.* PM Press.

Williams, R.N. (1971). *The new exiles: American war resisters in Canada.* Liveright Publishing.

Contributors

Alison is a professor of geography at the University of Toronto Scarborough, where she also serves as Vice-Principal, Research & Innovation. She researches how people cross borders, forge refuge, survive displacement, and resist war. She lives with her kids and dog and loves to write.

After tours in Iraq led him to refuse to return and desert instead, **Corey** crossed into Canada. In Toronto, he helped build a community for fellow resisters until facing deportation. He then journeyed abroad before political negotiations enabled his return to Canada, where he lives with his partner.

Dean, a Marine from upstate New York who enlisted in search of skills, financial stability, and access to higher education, left his military life behind after three post–9/11 tours in Iraq and Germany. Dean lives with PTSD and found healing and community in Toronto, where he lived with other resisters. Dean married, raised a family, and pursued his degree in electronics in Peterborough.

Esther and Dave's story is a love story as much as it is a story of resistance. Esther, who initially broke up with boyfriend Dave over his military enlistment, later rescued him from punitive detention as a war resister, fleeing with him to Canada, where she built a life of activism and nursing while helping him cope with severe PTSD. Dave succumbed to cancer in 2020. Esther continues to fight for social justice.

Joe is an American Los Angeleno and decorated medic from the war in Vietnam. He chose resistance over combat after witnessing war's realities, rebuilding his life in Canada where he served for 32 years as a judge while finding healing through martial arts and Buddhist practice.

John F., a Brooklyn native, chose Canada over military service in Vietnam in the late 1960s, transitioning from New York law student, through a brief period as Ontario banker, to Toronto law student. John eventually had a full legal career in Ontario while witnessing first-hand the era's shifting perspectives on war, gender, and social justice.

John S.'s journey from championship Missouri football player to Canadian war resister began with his opposition to racial violence and the war in Vietnam, leading him to the interior of British Columbia, where he built a multiracial family, worked as a teacher and school principal, and continues to document his resistance and his care for family and community.

Leah fled to Canada with her husband when her draft counselling work led to an arrest warrant. She then forged her own path from Montreal to British Columbia's Slocan Valley, where her activism evolved from religious roots to local politics.

Lee escaped service in Vietnam by fleeing to Toronto instead of declaring his sexuality. In Toronto he dedicated himself to community service and later helped guide a new generation of war resisters through the War Resisters Support Campaign. Lee died in 2024 and is remembered dearly by members of the WRSC and by the many resisters he welcomed to Canada.

Linjamin is a Black American who joined the military to escape homelessness after years in foster care. He resisted war in Iraq by fleeing to Canada as a war resister, finding healing in Toronto before being forced to confront America's racial inequalities upon his return. After marrying his wife in Russia, Linjamin returned to the United States with his family.

A socialist and queer activist in Toronto, **Michelle** was a co-founder of the War Resisters Support Campaign, which for 15 years advocated for US war resisters, engaging in political and legal battles and witnessing painful deportations. She lives with her partner and pet turtle and continues a lifelong struggle for social justice.

Neil fled military training at Fort Knox after being drafted into the war in Vietnam, journeying through several Canadian cities before finding himself in British Columbia's alternative communities, where his journey to resist paralleled his journey to come out as a gay man.

After fleeing to Canada as an Iraq War resister and building a new community there, **Robin** faced deportation in 2008 and a high-profile military trial resulting in 15 months' imprisonment, after which he continued his journey towards healing. Robin now lives in the United States.

Index

Page numbers in *italics* refer to maps and photographs.